REACHING *Your* DREAMS

TOMMY BARNETT

WITH JOEL KILPATRICK

REACHING *Your* DREAMS

Charisma
HOUSE
A STRANG COMPANY

Most STRANG COMMUNICATIONS/CHARISMA HOUSE/SILOAM products are available at special quantity discounts for bulk purchase for sales promotions, premiums, fund-raising, and educational needs. For details, write Strang Communications/Charisma House/Siloam, 600 Rinehart Road, Lake Mary, Florida 32746, or telephone (407) 333-0600.

REACHING YOUR DREAMS by Tommy Barnett with Joel Kilpatrick
Published by Charisma House
A Strang Company
600 Rinehart Road
Lake Mary, Florida 32746
www.charismahouse.com

Unless otherwise noted, all Scripture quotations are from the New King James Version of the Bible. Copyright © 1979, 1980, 1982 by Thomas Nelson, Inc., publishers. Used by permission.

Scripture quotations marked KJV are from the King James Version of the Bible.

Scripture quotations marked NAS are from the New American Standard Bible. Copyright © 1960, 1962, 1963, 1968, 1971, 1972, 1973, 1975, 1977 by the Lockman Foundation. Used by permission.

Scripture quotations marked NIV are from the Holy Bible, New International Version. Copyright © 1973, 1978, 1984, International Bible Society. Used by permission.

Cover design by Bill Henderson

Library of Congress Cataloging-in-Publication Data
Barnett, Tommy.
  Reaching your dreams / Tommy Barnett, Joel Kilpatrick.
    p. cm.
  ISBN 1-59185-640-X (pbk.)
  1. Dreams--Religious aspects--Christianity. 2. Success--Religious aspects-
-Christianity. 3. God--Will. 4. Self-actualization--Religious aspects--
Christianity. I. Kilpatrick, Joel. II. Title.
  BR115.D74B37 2005
  248.4--dc22
                                                2004026439
05 06 07 08 09 — 987654321
Printed in the United States of America

Contents

CHAPTER ONE

Discover Your Dream

*E*very one of us on Planet Earth was created by God to have a dream, a destiny, and a reason for living. When God created you, He needed something done on earth that nobody else could do, so He designed you to do it better than anyone else. There is a certain way you give love that nobody else can duplicate; a certain way you praise God that nobody else can imitate; a certain way you relate to people; a certain way you serve; a particular sense of humor you have; a particular way of singing, telling stories, building a business, designing, or decorating. You add something to this planet that nobody else can add. God receives special pleasure from you that He receives from nobody else.

That unique destiny, that dream, that special something you do better than anyone else is meant to change the course of earthly history. Each person has a moment when his or her dream and destiny can literally impact the lives of millions—perhaps billions—of people. You have probably heard the famous phrase about each person having "fifteen minutes of fame." That is a cynical reference to this fact: our dreams are meant to impact many other people. As you walk through life, you have preplanned appointments and opportunities to carry out your destiny in a way that will leave a mark on this planet forever. I don't care if your parents didn't plan your birth, or if you were made to feel unwanted as a child. Maybe you have been rejected as an adult or have lived a meaningless or self-serving life until now. You are on this planet for a reason, and that reason is found in your dream.

WHAT IS A DREAM?

By dreams I don't mean the nightly thoughts you experience as the brain sorts out the day's events. I am referring, rather, to the goals and visions that fire your heart and saturate your soul with joy at the very thought of them. I mean those continuing visions of what you want your life to be at its highest level of fulfillment—what you want to do, how you want to do it, what kind of person you want to become in the process. Your destiny and reason for living are wrapped up tightly in your dreams and desires, like the genetic information inside a seed. That dream in your heart contains your spiritual "DNA," the very blueprint for who you are. Your dream is that idea, that vision for your life that burns inside of you, something you can't tamp down or ignore for long. It keeps coming back to your mind because it is part of who you are; it will never leave you alone.

A dream doesn't *drive* you; it *draws* you. It is like a big magnet that pulls you toward itself.

There is no such thing as a man or woman without a dream, because God designed every member of the human race to have dreams. Dreams are the key to finding your fulfillment. Without a dream, a person will be frustrated in the present and will miss his or her future. It has been said, "No individual has the right to come into the world and go out of it without leaving behind him distinct and legitimate reasons for having passed through it." But most people have lost their dream. It seems impractical in this world to believe you were born for a destiny. Somehow it becomes more important to have a steady job, pay the mortgage, keep things moving forward with the least amount of disruption and the highest possibility for what our society calls "success."

Maybe you have been lured away from your dream. Maybe you believe your life is destined for insignificance. Somewhere along the way you got lost in the shuffle of humanity, out of God's sight. The Bible says He knew us from the foundation of the earth (Rev. 17:8). He had a purpose for us before we took our first breath. The Bible calls Him the "Great Shepherd," and we are the "sheep"; it says the Shepherd knows each of us by name. He knows your first name, your middle name, and your last name. He is personally familiar with you as an individual. God even told us, "I have inscribed you on the palms of My hands" (Isa. 49:16). God has tattooed your name on the palm of His hand if you are a professing Christian. He doesn't stop there: your name is on His lips, as He said, "I have *called* you by your name" (Isa. 43:1, emphasis added). And you are on His mind all the time, as David said, "The LORD has been mindful of us" (Ps. 115:12). He thinks about you. He dwells upon you. He puts your life before His eyes at every opportunity. We see a crowd at a sporting event, in a shopping mall, or in Times Square, and we see an indistinguishable mass of humanity. But He looks at a crowd and sees every person. To Him every face is different, every expression is a story, and every heart represents a dream bursting forth.

Every person longs to know that he or she has significance and meaning, and is unique and purposeful. I know a young man named Chalka who today works with us at our church in Los Angeles, but who once was a notorious graffiti artist. He wrote his name all over the Los Angeles area, along freeways, on buildings and billboards, on train stations, even in places that seemed unreachable. He single-handedly cost the City of Los Angeles $700,000 as they cleaned up after him.

Then the Lord saved him and brought him to us. One day while we were working, I said to him, "Chalka, why did you write your name everywhere?"

He said, "Because I felt lost in this big city. I felt so unimportant. When I saw my name all over town it gave me a certain prominence. I needed to have some identity."

Each person feels that same way. We want to fulfill our God-given desire to change the world. We want to be great, and we can only be great if we fulfill our dreams.

How to Know Your Dream Is From God

Where do dreams come from? From your own imagination? Your parents? Your boss? Your spouse? Your upbringing or a favorite teacher? No, dreams don't come from men. Your dream did not even originate with you. It resides within you, but God put it there. He is the source of your dream.

When people dream without God, they find it hollow and unsatisfying. Every person must come to Jesus for his or her dream to make sense. In fact, without Jesus, you might follow a dream for your life that God never put in your heart. Not every dream is from God. Some people dream of being rich and having wild parties, so their dream drives them into an unrestrained, reckless lifestyle. Other people dream of cheating people out of their money or wooing unsuspecting people into romantic relationships. Those are godless dreams.

But when your dream is God's dream, it's unstoppable. The very first step to reaching your dream is to begin a relationship with Christ. He created the world we live in and foresaw each one of us. He put a plan in place to reunite us with God. He died to save us, and He reconnected dreamers—you and me—with our dream-giver, God. Jesus said that apart from Him we can't do anything and that all our dreams will be frustrated. He said He is the vine and we are the branches. Branches only grow and produce fruit when connected to the vine. So the power, energy, and creativity needed to fulfill our dreams must flow from Jesus.

Once you have a relationship with Christ, you can begin to sort through your dreams and decide which ones are from God. The most common and most crucial question is, "How do I know which dreams in my heart are from God?" Here is the answer. You will know it's God's dream if:

1. It is bigger than you.

2. You can't let it go.

3. You would be willing to give everything for it.

4. It will last forever.

5. It meets a need nobody else has met.

6. It brings glory to God.

Let's go through each of these. First, any dream God put in your heart will be much bigger than you. Most children start out with big dreams of being a major league baseball player or the first woman president of the United States. But people and circumstances whittle those dreams down to size. We reach adulthood, and we voluntarily trim our dreams to manageable proportions so we won't be disappointed.

That's the opposite of what we should do. We should set higher goals, not lower ones. God is the author of bigness, not littleness. We may not reach the highest dream, but we will go a lot farther by aiming high than aiming low. The first test you can apply to your dream is: "Is it too big for me to fulfill without God's help?" If you can do it without His help, you are not dreaming big enough. If it's much bigger than you, you are on the right track! The Bible promises that all things are possible with God. Is your dream impossible enough? Does it go beyond you enough to qualify for God's help? Your dream should be so big that it takes your breath away, makes you temporarily weak in the knees, and makes you cry out to God for help and guidance.

Next, are you able to let this dream go, or does it keep bugging you? A God-given dream is a bothersome thing: it won't leave you alone! It keeps bobbing to the surface of your heart, clamoring for your mind's attention. If that's how your dream behaves, then it is probably from God.

You also know it's a God-given dream if you are willing to devote every ounce of energy and every minute of your days to it. A dream inspires devotion like the devotion a parent has for a child: you would give your very life just to see it grow and find fulfillment.

The next way to know it's God-given is if your dream will last forever. Many people pursue dreams built on things that will fade away. They dream of fame, but fame never lasts. Yesterday's big star is today's trivia punch line. You're a hero today and a zero tomorrow.

Others build dreams on wealth, health, or power, but none of these last more than a few decades at most. A dream cannot be built on ego. People sniff out ego trips quicker than anything. It cannot be built on tradition—because the company expects it or your family expects it. None of these foundations will support your dream.

You have to build your dreams on something that will last. The Bible—God's handbook—says only two things in the entire world will last forever: truth and people. The Bible says heaven and earth will pass away, but God's Word will never pass away. Think about that; even heaven will one day become obsolete, but truth will last forever. Where is truth found? In God's Word, the Bible. You have to build your dream on that never-changing foundation, which is why it's so important to read from the Bible often. We'll talk about that later.

The second thing that lasts forever is people. God made human beings to last forever. They never pass away. Jesus came to seek and save that which was lost, to die for people. That's how we should spend our lives, too. If God Himself thought people were worth dying for, shouldn't we follow His example? In fact, the only way to minister to God is to minister to people, as He said, "When you've done it to the least of them, you've done it to Me." (See Matthew 24:40.) Your dream must be built on human need. Will it help people? Improve lives? Alleviate human suffering? Does it fill a need nobody else is filling? If so, you can be sure that dream is from God. People are often like empty vessels you pour into. You don't need to expect much out of them; just be thankful you have someone to pour into. The secret to happiness in life is pouring into other people, giving without expecting anything in return. We'll talk about that later, too.

Finally, your dream should bring glory to God. The most horrible thing in life is to realize you have wasted months, years, or decades following the wrong dream. Life is too precious to fritter away by building on a crumbling foundation. Many people lose their lives, not by dying, but by squandering their time.

GREAT PEOPLE FOLLOW THEIR DREAMS

The greatest men and women in biblical history followed the dreams God placed in their hearts. Noah was able to build an ark in spite of the scoffing of his day. Why? Because he had a dream.

- Abraham was able to leave his father and his friends and go to a new land because he had a dream and a destiny.

- Joseph was able to endure persecution, imprisonment, and lying because he had a dream.

- Moses was willing to leave the palace and the riches of Egypt because he had a God-given dream.

- David confounded the giant and led a nation to greatness because he had a dream.

- Daniel was able to stay in the lions' den because he had a dream.

- Stephen took the stoning because he lived for his dream. Paul was shipwrecked, beaten, and stoned, but he continued on because of his dream.

- Jesus Christ, the Son of the living God, was willing to leave His home in glory and come to a world that hated Him. He was able to endure the cross and endure the shame. Why? Because He had a dream that all who would accept Him would live with Him forever.

God takes pleasure in our dreams. You are unique and uniquely important in His plan for humanity. You are not one in a million; you're one in eight billion. When you get to heaven, God won't say, "Why weren't you more like Billy Graham, or Moses, or the apostle Paul?" He may very well say, "Why weren't you more like you? Did you follow your dream to the end?"

DISCOVERING YOUR DREAM

A dream is of no use unless it's discovered, just as gold is of no use unless it's mined from the ground. Have you ever discovered and defined your dream? Do you know for a fact the distinct reason God put you upon this earth? If not, then these six steps will help you discover and define it.

1. Get alone with God.

One reason why people never discover their dream and purpose in life is because they never stop long enough to listen. They are like the World War II pilot who became lost over the ocean and radioed back, "I have no idea where I am or where I'm heading, but I'm making record time." Someone else said, "It's an ironic habit of the human race that we double our speed when we've lost our way."

We have to get alone with God and listen. Psalm 46:10 says, "Be still, and know that I am God." To get a vision from God, turn off the television. Get quiet. Let God talk to you. An Indian tribe in Oregon used to send young men out, when they came of age, with the instruction, "Don't come back until you have a vision." Those who got discouraged came back early. Those who stayed until they had a vision became the leaders of the tribe.

Paul spent three years in the desert listening to God before he began his ministry. That was his seminary education. He said, "God, what is the overarching, all-consuming passion of my life? What will I do until I die?" Once he discovered his dream, he lived an extraordinary life.

2. Next, review your gifts and talents.

Romans 12:6 says we each have gifts. God gave you the gifts you have; you didn't choose them. Fulfillment comes when you use those gifts for Him in service of your dream. Your gifts are the key to discovering God's will in your life. What are your abilities? What do you like to do? God uses our desires to identify what we should do. Desire points us to our dreams. God uses desire to accomplish what He wants on this earth. How did He make sure the world was populated? He gave men and women a desire for each other to produce children. How did he make sure we cared for our bodies? He made us thirsty and made two-thirds of the planet water. He made us hungry and caused food to grow all around us.

God speaks to us through desires. Many Christians have come to think that their motives and desires are corrupt and untrustworthy, but the Bible says that if any man is in Christ Jesus, he is a new creature. Old things pass away, and all things become new (2 Cor. 5:17). That includes our desires! The Bible says you can have the mind of Christ within you. So what does it say about your desires? It says your desires, when you become a new creature, are changed. That's why God can say, "I want to give you the desires of your heart."

3. Review your experience.

We pay attention not only to our desires and talents, but also to our past history. This is a powerful thing. Romans 8:28 says, "All things work together for good." God uses all things. Perhaps you were taught a certain skill as a young person, like playing the piano or building houses. Those skills are useful to God. He may want you to use them further in your life. Perhaps you were raised in another country and learned to speak a language other than English. Maybe you have experience in international travel, counseling, or business that might become part of your dream. God can use those to serve your larger goals. Even if it's a skill you don't particularly enjoy, you may find it opens doors for you at key times.

Not everything in our past is bound to be good. Some people reading this may have lingering pain in their lives. Some went through a divorce, grew up with angry parents, or struggled with alcohol. Some had abortions, filed for bankruptcy, or endured hurts that cannot be easily explained. But each of these problems falls into the category of "all things." God wants to integrate your hurts and difficulties into your life message. He never wastes circumstances, even bad ones. Before you became a believer, God was working to redeem the problems you faced. Not all things are good, but all things will work for the good of those who love Him and are called according to His purpose (Rom. 8:28).

Even more than that, God will give you a special ability to minister to people who are going through what you went through. Second Corinthians 1:4 says God helps us in our troubles so we can help others who have troubles, using the same help we ourselves have received from God. When you grasp that, it will change the way you view your life circumstances, and it will help you discover your dream.

4. Decide what's really important in life.

Paul wrote in 1 Corinthians 10:23, "All things are lawful for me, but not all things are helpful." Some things are not necessarily wrong, but they're just not necessary. They waste time. We might not have time to pursue every dream, so we must choose to spend time on what's important. Successful people learn to eliminate nonessentials, those things that won't matter ten years from now. We saw earlier that only two things will last forever, truth and people. Invest your life in those things that will outlast you.

5. Begin to explore different avenues.

If you have done these things and still don't know in what direction your dreams are taking you, begin to explore. Try out different ministries, business avenues, and educational possibilites. Take classes; volunteer until something sparks. You will find your place much quicker if you are actively participating.

6. Journal your dream.

Once you are able to define your dream, write it down. Habakkuk 2:2 says, "Then the LORD answered me and said: 'Write the vision and make it plain on tablets, that he may run who reads it.'"

If you want to move ahead in your dream, you must write it down—inscribe it indelibly. That shows resolve, definition, and form. It is not enough to have an idea of what you want to do; you must have a plan for implementing it. Dreams do not come true by fantasizing—you have to write them down and let them become a guiding force in your life.

If there was one gift I could give to you, it would be the gift of vision, of seeing what God designed your life to be. Romans 15:20 says, "I have made it my aim to preach the gospel, not where Christ was named." Ambition is not wrong if it flows from a godly pursuit of your dream. Paul put his ambition in preaching the gospel. Later on, in Acts 26:19, Paul said, "I was not disobedient to the heavenly vision." Your dream is more than a goal; it's a clearly defined objective for your existence.

Every person ought to define his or her life in one word. When people think of Tiger Woods, they think *golf*. When they think of Steven Spielberg, they think *movies*. When they think of Imelda Marcos, they think *shoes* or the *Philippines*.

What word pops into your mind when you think of your husband? *Television? La-Z-Boy? Sports?* How about your wife? *Shopping?* Heaven forbid—*jewelry?*

How do you want to be defined? Why not *integrity, servant,* or perhaps *soulwinner, giver, or discipler?*

Study Guide Questions

1. When did you first begin to understand what your dream and destiny in life are?

    _____

    _____

    _____

    _____

2. If you are still discovering your dream, how do you intend to go about achieving it? Are you getting alone with God so that you hear from Him? Are you trying out different things to discover what you have a passion for? Sketch a personal plan of action for discovering your dream.

    _____

    _____

    _____

    _____

3. What are the most important talents, skills, and experiences in your life? How do these point you to your dream? Explain.

    _____

    _____

    _____

    _____

4.   Is your dream bigger than you? Why do you believe it will last forever?

_____

_____

_____

_____

5.   Does your dream meet a need nobody else has met? Explain.

_____

_____

_____

_____

6.   Have you ever tried to let your dream go? What happened?

_____

_____

_____

_____

7. Pick a word you hope will define your life. Write it below. What word would friends, family, and co-workers choose to describe you? Write down what you think they would say.

_____

_____

_____

_____

Reflections

Day 1

Read and review the chapter material.

Day 2

> Where there is no vision, the people perish.
>
> —Proverbs 29:18, KJV

Have you ever fallen out of shape? I have. A few years ago I was so busy traveling and preaching that I had no time for exercise. My body grew lazy and sluggish, and I felt terrible and unfocused in my mind. I needed a goal, a vision for getting back into shape. That vision included a dream I had suppressed. I had always wanted to run all the way across the United States. While I couldn't devote the months to running that far, I could run the four hundred or so miles from Phoenix to Los Angeles.

I grabbed hold of that dream, and it revitalized me! I trained hard, got my body and mind in good condition, and spent my two-week vacation running across the desert to raise money for my church in Los Angeles. That run was one of the toughest—and yet most fulfilling—experiences of my life. The sky was clear, the air was fresh, and there were no phone calls or appointments.

The worst part was crossing the finish line, because the adventure ended!

That dream helped me rediscover my vision for staying mentally and physically fit. In the same way, each of us must discover and pursue the larger dream God has built into our lives. God created you to dream. When you have no dream, you wander in circles, get "out of shape," and the dream eventually perishes. Hardship and affliction have never broken a person, but living without a dream ruins people all the time.

A life-defining, life-sustaining dream must be an essential part of your everyday life. Don't wait to discover that you have grown out of shape and are directionless. Set your course now in the direction of your dream.

1. What is your "dream fitness" level? Are you in good shape, or have you grown slow and lazy in pursuing your dream? Give an honest written assessment of yourself:

    _____

    _____

    _____

    _____

Consider Habakkuk 2:2:

> Then the LORD answered me and said: "Write the vision and make it plain on tablets, that he may run who reads it."

2. What is your dream, very specifically? What vision are you pursuing? Journal your dream.

    _____

    _____

    _____

    _____

DAY 3

But we have this treasure in jars of clay to show that this all-surpassing power is from God and not from us.

—2 CORINTHIANS 4:7, NIV

Not long ago a woman in our city who was known as a "bag lady" died. Everybody thought she was flat broke, but when people retrieved her body at her home, they found trash cans full of money and cash stuffed under carpets and hidden in many other places. She was worth millions, but her treasure remained hidden and unused.

You too have a dream within you that is worth more than the gold in Fort Knox. It is a hidden treasure inside of you. So the question is not whether you know that you have treasure within you, but whether you are putting that treasure to use. Perhaps your dream would help the poor, create a new business, invent a product, or change the world in other ways. But is your dream hidden and dormant, or are you putting it to work?

The Bible warns against keeping our treasure to ourselves. Jesus told a story about three men who received money to invest. Two of them put the money to work, and when the master came back, they were rewarded. But the third man hid his money in the ground, and the master took his "treasure" away and banished him from his presence. (See Matthew 25:14–30.)

God gave you your dream for a specific reason. He wants you to use it to change the world, to bring glory to Him, and to accomplish something that will last forever.

What treasure lies within you? God knows the answer. He sees your dream clearly, even if you have not fully discovered it yet. You have within you a hope and a God-given future, a dream that will guide you toward your destiny. None of us should delay in discovering that treasure inside of us and putting it to work. Don't let life slip by while the treasure remains hidden away. Begin today to discover your God-given purpose.

1. How do you judge now whether your dream is active or inactive in your life?

     _____

     _____

     _____

     _____

2. How would your life be different if you were fully pursuing your dream?

     _____

     _____

     _____

     _____

DAY 4

> There is none like you, O Lord; no deeds can compare with yours....For you are great and do marvelous deeds; you alone are God.
>
> —PSALM 86:8, 10, NIV

Some people start dreaming big at a young age, like Joseph from the Book of Genesis. He dreamed so big that when he shared it with his brothers, they mocked and resented him for it. He dreamed that one day he would be a great leader and his brothers would bow to him. He held on to that big dream even when he was sold to slave traders and unjustly sent to prison. He was one of those people who naturally dream big, in spite of the circumstances.

Is that you? How big is your dream? Are you dreaming so big that other people find it incredible? Impossible? Amazing?

Good! You're on the right track. The Bible says many times that God's deeds are great, awesome, marvelous, and too wonderful for us to fully comprehend. He is a God of bigness, boldness, of great things.

But others of us are like Gideon, who dreamed smaller than God did. Gideon had the kind of personality that saw the glass as half empty; he saw what couldn't be instead of what could be. But God didn't let him get away with dreaming small. One day an angel showed up and surprised Gideon by saying:

> The LORD is with you, mighty warrior.
>
> —JUDGES 6:12

Gideon responded by protesting:

> My clan is the weakest in Manasseh, and I am the least in my father's house.
>
> —JUDGES 6:15

Does that sound like you? Do you cling to small dreams, even when God wants to bring big dreams to pass for you? Are you always reducing what He wishes to do?

The good news is that God is in the business of drawing us back to our big dreams. Like Gideon, we really can become mighty warriors, and when we relentlessly pursue our dream, the results will be beyond what we could have hoped. Because Gideon allowed his dream to grow, "the land enjoyed peace forty years" (Judg. 8:28, NIV).

Those are big results from a man who initially was full of doubt. But that just goes to show that God gives no small dreams.

Consider these verses:

> Now to him who is able to do immeasurably more than all we ask or imagine, according to his power that is at work within us, to him be glory in the church and in Christ Jesus throughout all generations, for ever and ever! Amen.
> —EPHESIANS 3:20–21, NIV

> I tell you the truth, anyone who has faith in me will do what I have been doing. He will do even greater things than these, because I am going to the Father.
> —JOHN 14:12, NIV

1. Are you dreaming big enough? How can you tell? Explain.

_____

_____

_____

_____

Day 5

> Very early in the morning, while it was still dark, Jesus got up, left the house and went off to a solitary place, where he prayed.
>
> —Mark 1:35, niv

A friend of mine was listening to the radio while driving during a long trip. He was listening to a preacher whose message was, "God loves you so much." Then the signal from that station began to weaken and gave way to another station that was stronger. It was a music station playing a rock-and-roll song that said, "You're no good…baby, you're no good." He drove a little further, and the station with the preacher came back; so he heard, "God loves you so much." Then the rock-and-roll station took over again: "You're no good…baby, you're no good."

Talk about mixed signals!

Have you ever felt your attention going in two directions? Have the voices of people around you drowned out your dream? Some people live like my friend, going back and forth between different voices saying opposite things. God's voice tells them, "Keep following that dream! I love it when you go after the destiny I planned for you from before time began." Other voices say, "That dream is pie in the sky. Quit wasting time. Get practical!"

Have you had trouble making up your mind whom you're listening to? Here's the solution: get alone with God so you can hear His encouragement. Jesus did it while He was on earth. Luke 5:16 tells us:

> Jesus often withdrew to lonely places and prayed.
>
> —niv

Then it says in the next verse that when He returned to His task, "the power of the Lord was present for him to heal the sick" (v. 17, NIV).

The power of your dream springs from time spent in solitude with God, listening to His voice and forgetting all other distractions.

1. Why do you think people need to spend time alone with God? What happens in those transactions? Explain.

    _____

    _____

    _____

    _____

2. When did you last spend time alone with God? What was that time like? How were you different afterward?

    _____

    _____

    _____

    _____

3.   Do you fear getting alone with God because of what you've done or what He might say? Do you ever feel awkward, ashamed, or self-conscious in His presence? Explain.

_____

_____

_____

_____

4.   How often do you need alone time with God? In the space below write down a weekly schedule that would serve you best.

	Morning	Evening
Sunday		
Monday		
Tuesday		
Wednesday		
Thursday		
Friday		
Saturday		

DAY 6

David said to Saul, "Your servant has been keeping his father's sheep. When a lion or a bear came and carried off a sheep from the flock, I went after it, struck it and

rescued the sheep from its mouth. When it turned on
me, I seized it by its hair, struck it and killed it. Your
servant has killed both the lion and the bear; this
uncircumcised Philistine [Goliath] will be like one
of them."

—1 SAMUEL 17:34–36, NIV

As you start to define your dream, your talents and experiences should help you a great deal. For example, if you are naturally gifted in the areas of finances, music, or public speaking,
those gifts will point you in those directions, as they should.
Paul said:

We have different gifts, according to the grace given us.
—ROMANS 12:6, NIV

The gifts and talents we have are not happenstance; God gives
them. Everybody has gifts. We should pay attention to them. They
are a big part of our dreams.

We should also pay attention to any skills we have developed
and any life experiences that endow us with certain knowledge
or expertise. When David saw the opportunity to fight the giant
Goliath, he emboldened himself by remembering how he won
previous "impossible" battles against wild animals. His experience and skill in close combat made him unafraid. That is what
we must do when pursuing our dreams.

Maybe you are one of those people who say, "I'm not good at
anything." Hogwash! Everybody is good at something. Everybody
has natural gifts and life experiences. The Bible says, "Each man
has his own gift from God; one has this gift, another has that" (1
Cor. 7:7, NIV).

Perhaps you haven't put enough effort into discovering what you are good at. Or maybe your talents are so obvious that you don't see them anymore. In any case, having a clear idea of your past experience and talents will speed you toward your dream.

1. What are you good at? What important experiences have you had? How does this relate to your dream, if at all? Explain.

    _____

    _____

    _____

    _____

2. Have you ever thought, *I'm not good at anything?* If so, now is the time to repent for leaving your God-given gifts unnoticed or unused. Write a prayer asking God to help you see your gifts and talents.

    _____

    _____

    _____

    _____

DAY 7

> So we fix our eyes not on what is seen, but on what is unseen. For what is seen is temporary, but what is unseen is eternal.
>
> —2 CORINTHIANS 4:18, NIV

When I was a young man, I saved $5,000 of hard-earned money and decided to invest it with the help of a man who said he could make that investment grow. But within a few months, he invested poorly, didn't really tend to it, and lost it all. I was so sick about the loss that I almost had ulcers.

I never got that money back, but I learned a number of lessons that served me far better than money. One of them was *invest in what lasts.*

Did you know that the dollar in your purse or pocket is declining in value, even as you read this? Almost everything you own is worth far less than what you spent on it. Very few things tend to increase in value. Land is one; fine art and stocks are others. But even these have a short shelf life when compared with eternity. And no investment on earth is certain.

Where should you invest your money, your life, and your dream? Jesus gave the best advice:

> Do not store up for yourselves treasures on earth, where moth and rust destroy, and where thieves break in and steal. But store up for yourselves treasures in heaven, where moth and rust do not destroy, and where thieves do not break in and steal.
>
> —MATTHEW 6:19–20, NIV

The only things that last forever are truth and people. Jesus told us:

> Heaven and earth will pass away, but my words will never pass away.
>
> —MATTHEW 24:35, NIV

He also said:

> I am the living bread that came down from heaven. If anyone eats of this bread, he will live forever.
>
> —JOHN 6:51, NIV

Those who don't serve Jesus "will go away to eternal punishment, but the righteous to eternal life" (Matt. 25:46, NIV).

If your dream is built on anything but the truth and people, it will last only a short time. Ask yourself: "Is the primary purpose of my dream to serve others? Does it meet a need nobody else is meeting? Does it alleviate suffering and improve life for people?"

If so, that's a dream to follow!

1.   What are the benefits your dream will bring to other people? List them:

   _____

   _____

   _____

   _____

2. How fixed are your eyes on things that are eternal? What are the biggest distractions? Television? Anxieties? Relationships? List them:

_____

_____

_____

_____

Pray and ask God to help you invest your life in ways that will reap eternal benefits.

CHAPTER TWO

What Is Holding You Back?

*T*o dream, to really live, means overcoming our own excuses and the barriers that confront us as we move toward our destiny. Some people get stuck on the way because of events in their past or obstacles that seem immovable. Other people are afraid of following their dream, so they employ avoidance techniques, busy schedules, and willful ignorance to try to drown out the voice in their heart that whispers, "You should be following your dream."

I have identified vital signs that tell you if you're not following your dream. See if any of them apply to you.

YOU ARE DEFINED BY YOUR PAST

A person without a future will always return to his or her past. He or she will always go back to old friends, old hangouts, old habits, trying to find meaning.

In the Bible, Judas lost sight of his dream, so he went back to his old habits of cheating people and making a quick buck…this time by selling the Master for thirty pieces of silver.

Peter's dream was crushed when Jesus was crucified, so he left town and went back to his old occupation: fishing.

Many people today call up old friends or drive by old haunts when they get discouraged. But when you are drawn to your past, it is because your dream has stopped drawing you to your future. Only a dream can give you the booster rockets to escape the gravity of the past. Only a dream gives you daily motivation to go forward, to keep your priorities straight, to help you distinguish between what belongs in the past and what belongs in the future.

Did you know we have God's permission to forget the past? He gives us the option to leave yesterday behind. If we don't, we will remain paralyzed by the past, even the good parts of our past. To reach our dreams we must learn to practice selective memory.

When I was a young man, I left my hometown of Kansas City to pastor a church in Davenport, Iowa. That was a tough assignment: the elders were grumpy, and the finances nonexistent. To keep myself encouraged, I nurtured a strong affection for Kansas City. I put my Kansas City Chiefs pennant on the wall. I ate Kansas City steaks. I always ran home to Kansas City when I had a chance, and I would talk about Kansas City at any opportunity. As a consequence, I was always homesick for Kansas City.

One day God spoke to me and said, "Burn the pennant, quit eating Kansas City steaks, and don't go back and visit anymore.

That's all in the past." I obeyed, and that day I began to learn the value of selective memory.

You see, some people never let go of their past, and so they live in yesterday's memories. These people get their scrapbooks out and take you down memory lane whenever you visit them. It's as if they are in a former era in their minds. Someone asked me one time if they could see my scrapbook. I told him, "I don't have a scrapbook because I'm too busy making scrap."

Are you stuck in memories of the past, whether good or bad? Do you still think about that past relationship, and you can't sleep at night? Or do you pine for the "good times" you had way back when? It's time for you to sit down and identify which memories are holding you back, and then selectively "forget" them. Refuse to bring them up, if you can help it. Paul said, "…forgetting those things which are behind" (Phil. 3:13). He was talking about the bad things *and* the good things in his past. He selectively forgot them both, because his dream mattered more to him.

UNFINISHED BUSINESS

Some people have many wonderful things in their lives—friends, family, wealth, vacations, and retirement security—but they feel incomplete. They have a nagging sense of unfinished business because they have not reached their full capacity by achieving their dream.

Some people reading these very words will feel like crying, and might even become desperate, and they won't know exactly why. Such weeping often comes unannounced for you and for no apparent reason. Oh sure, we all get tired at times, but this is something more significant. It springs up from hidden wells of disappointment within you. I have a suggestion: Perhaps the tears flow because there is unfinished business in your life. Perhaps in the depths of your soul you know that you are neglecting your dream, missing your moment, putting your purpose in a drawer for a later time that never comes. The Bible identifies this as "double-mindedness" and says it will make you unstable in all your ways (James 1:8). You won't really accomplish anything lasting. Even though your life may look stable, there is a deep fissure between who you are and who you know you ought to be, and it creates below-the-surface instability. How much disunity do we create in our families and in our own minds because of the untended dreams lying dormant at the bottom of our souls?

If you have a constant, aching sense of unfinished business, you are probably avoiding your dream. You might also find yourself suffering from the following negative symptoms.

Boredom and self-destruction

When you lose sight of your dream, boredom sets in—deep, pervasive boredom and unsettledness—and in the midst of apparent success it drives you to the hollow pursuit of pleasure and leisure. People even drink, have illicit affairs, gamble money away, wrap their lives up in sports, and do drugs because they become bored. They have lost touch with their dream and their future.

Proverbs 29:18 says, "Where there is no revelation, the people cast off restraint." Where there is no God-given dream, people cast off restraint. In their boredom, they go anywhere and do anything for a thrill. There's nothing to hold them back. Why not have extramarital affairs? Why not spend foolishly?

One time I picked up a young hitchhiker. I don't normally do that, but it was pouring rain, and I felt that maybe this young man needed help, so I pulled over and invited him into the warm car. He seemed bored, directionless, and depressed. I asked where he was going, and he said, "No place in particular." I probed further and asked what his goals in life were. He looked at me and said, "Mister, you don't get it. I'm not going anywhere." He asked to be let out, and away he walked in the rain.

That young man is symbolic of how some live their lives. They walk along the highway with their thumb out, waiting to catch a ride with anyone who will stop. They are bored. They will go literally anywhere. They don't care.

People need a sense that they exist for a reason. They need the clarity that a dream brings. Where there is no dream, there is no order to life, no reason to live. We perish by confusion and disorder; we make a mess of everything.

If you are bored and beginning to experiment with behavior you know will harm you, or even just cultivating pastimes you know are a waste of time, you have lost sight of your dream.

Disappointment

Sometimes you dream, and that dream is shattered. The experience creates a deep wound in your heart that gets filled with disappointment, like a bitter well. You approach each new opportunity with melancholy and doubt stored up inside of you. The waters from that well blur your vision and obscure your dream, and the disappointment grows more potent the longer you hang on to it. It stops being a well and becomes a wide river separating you from your dream.

Moses endured one of the greatest disappointments in the Bible. He spent forty years leading the children of Israel through the desert, doing everything so well, obeying God when the others were worshiping a golden calf. He didn't grumble as they did or doubt God, but because he disobeyed God on one occasion when his anger got the better of him, the Lord forbade him from going into the

Promised Land. The Lord even took him to a mountaintop where Moses saw the magnificent reality of the Promised Land (Deut. 34:1). He had the thrill of drinking it in with his own eyes, but he had to live with the stunning reality that he would never touch it.

Nothing hurts quite like disappointment. The word implies that we believed we had an appointment, but when we got there, things didn't happen the way we wanted them to. We were "dis-appointed." Our momentary assessment of a situation is always affected by human limitations. We cannot always see what God sees, and much more may be happening than we aware of. The Bible says we see through a veil; our knowledge is imperfect. At some point, you have to give your disappointment to God and trust His judgment, which is perfect. What seems like a disappointment may have been the best thing to happen in your life. That relationship that ended, that business opportunity you passed by, that investment you didn't make—God may have been sparing you.

Even if you believe you have good reason to be disappointed, you should have a better reason for letting disappointment go. That reason is your dreams. There will be bitter disappointments in life. People will drop the ball, lead you astray, abandon you, and worse. You will be disappointed with God. But if you want to reach your dreams, you must become an expert in releasing disappointments.

Oversatisfaction

Satisfaction is also the enemy of a dream. Some look at their life and pronounce it good enough. They hit the cruise control button and lean back instead of forging ahead. They become satisfied with slow, incremental progress. Instead of being drawn by a dream, they are drawn to enjoy the abundance God gave them, so they spend time planning vacations, buying recreational equipment, and turning a blind eye to their higher calling. They trade their dream for the pleasantness of present circumstances. Some ride this satisfaction to the very end of their life.

Fear of the battles

Some people fear the battle so much that they abandon their dreams before they ever reach the battlefield; they never even try, or they give up quickly. I'll be the first one to say that following your dream is agonizing, especially in the beginning. But fear of the battle causes some people to stay stuck at the starting gate forever. They are waiting for some mystical wave of emotional energy to propel them effortlessly through difficulties, problems, and crises. But that approach just doesn't square with reality. Life is full of battles, no matter which course we take. It is no different when we follow our dreams.

But the battle itself is always less frightening than the days leading up to it. Anticipation will kill you quicker than the fighting! When I face battles, I feel weakest before the battle even starts. I know God will see me through the battle, but sometimes I wonder if He will see me *to* the battle. I rarely have peace before the battle. Rather, I feel overwhelmed, powerless, and ineffective. Maybe you know what I mean. You have gone through surgery and were afraid up until the moment they wheeled you into the operating room. Maybe you competed in a contest and dreaded every second until you stepped up to take your turn. Maybe you started a business and laid yourself on the line, wondering if it would pay off. What does this tell us about pursuing our dreams? There will seldom be that moment of absolute conviction of victory as we embark on the dream path. If you wait for people to toss flowers at your feet and wish you success, you will be waiting a long time. Yet fear of the battle stops many people in their tracks, frozen to the spot as their opportunities slip away.

Have Courage!

Courage isn't just for comic book heroes and movie stars. It's for anyone who will go after his or her dream. Life is going to be full of battles, no matter what. But when you dream, the battles are taking you somewhere. I am not a fighter by nature. I don't like fighting, and maybe you don't either. I would rather be a peace-maker and follow my dreams outside the fray. But life is short, and the enemy strives against my dreams. I have come to realize that battle is the normal way of life. I have even grown to enjoy the rigors of battle because I know that once I'm in it, God will fight with me.

The Bible spurs me on when it talks about courageous people who "by faith conquered kingdoms, performed acts of righteous-ness, obtained promises, shut the mouths of lions, quenched the power of fire, escaped the edge of the sword" (Heb. 11:33–34, NAS). I love those action words: *conquered, obtained, escaped.* Those are words of courage and reward. Promises must be obtained, king-doms must be conquered, the lions' mouths must be shut. And the best part, I believe, is that these people became powerful in battle, not before it. Courage gets you *to* the battle. God's power sees you *through* the battle.

I have noticed that God never supplies power until I need it. He always provides power along the way, after I have decided to go in the direction of a dream. You have to take steps toward your dream before you will receive power to fulfill it. God promises that you can do all things through Christ who gives you strength (Phil. 4:13). That should give you courage. The example of Jesus should give you courage. He agonized in the Garden of Gethsemane the night before He was crucified. He knew what the next thirty-six hours held for Him. He would suffer as no man has suffered before or since. The human side of Him screamed out in protest, "I can't do it. Let this cup pass from Me." But after a time of prayer and surrender, He got up and said, "Rise, let us be going." And He walked in the direction of His betrayer.

That took courage. The dream of saving humanity shone brighter than the battle it would take to achieve it. And on the way to the cross, God provided the power Jesus needed to see His task to the end.

The decision to follow your dream is often made in quiet places, in the middle of the night, with no fanfare or celebration, and with a deep sense of impending doom. Many times I have lain awake at night literally sweating with fear because of a decision I had to make.

That is where you summon your courage. You may see the battle rising, the clouds gathering, and the enemies arrayed before you. Instead of abandoning your post or going back to a life defined by other people's opinions, dig in and get ready to fight for your dream. Walk with courage in the direction of your calling. God will supply power along the way.

I have discovered an amazing fact: if you hold on to a dream for about five years, it will come to pass. Most people cannot keep a dream for that long. Discouragement and failure wear on them, and they surrender the dream. But if you stick with it through the battles, the disappointments, and the failures, you will experience a glorious transition. At first you had to hang on to the dream, but suddenly the dream begins to hang on to you. You won't be able to let it go if you wanted to. At first you had to work on the dream, but now it works on you, changing your character. Dreams make an ordinary person great, if you break free of the past to pursue them.

Learn From Failure

If you have failed on the way to your dream due to an error or misjudgment, move on and don't let it affect you. Every dreamer misses the mark at times, but successful dreamers know that failure is not fatal. Some people exaggerate the effects of failure on their life. They blow it out of proportion. Their reaction to failure does far more damage than the failure itself.

I believe that the more talented you are, the more you tend to fear failure. Maybe it's because you understand the risks better, or maybe it's because you have more to lose. But when former failure rules your life, it is impossible to pursue your dreams. Failure should not ever derail you. Proverbs 24:16 says, "For a righteous man may fall seven times and rise again." I love this passage because it tells us there's nothing wrong with being down, but there is something wrong with staying down. Even good guys make mistakes. The difference between successful people and unsuccessful people is that successful people don't get derailed by failure. They get back on track and keep going.

To reach our dreams, we must redefine failure. Failure is not stumbling on the way to your dream. Failure is not having a dream at all. Failure isn't flubbing the opportunity; it's not taking the opportunity in the first place.

I read about a famous "failure" named George Washington, who lost two-thirds of all the battles he fought. Another failure was Babe Ruth, who hit 714 home runs during his career and struck out 1,333 times—twice as often as he hit a home run. I like what he said about failure: "Never let the fear of striking out keep you from swinging at the ball."

R. P. Macy, founder of Macy's department store, failed seven times at retailing before he succeeded with Macy's and made billions of dollars.

Success doesn't come by never failing; it comes by repetition. You try and fail, and try and fail, and try and try until you succeed. In fact, failure is one of the primary tools God uses to develop your dream and your character. People rarely learn anything from success. They simply think, *I have a lot of talent and ability. Look what I pulled off.* Most people don't take time to figure out why they succeeded. But you can learn magnificent lessons from your failure.

God uses failure to educate us.

Mistakes and success are partners; they work together. Psalm 119:71 says, "It is good for me that I have been afflicted, that I may learn Your statutes." There is no such thing as success without mistakes.

God uses failure to motivate us.

When you find yourself knocked down, with dirt ground into your knees and palms, it should strengthen your resolve to get up and try even harder. Nobody wants to fail again. Nobody likes that experience. That should motivate you to learn and do better next time.

God uses failure to cultivate our character and refine our dreams.

Romans 5:3–4 says, "We also glory in tribulations, knowing that tribulation produces perseverance; and perseverance, character." What kind of character are we talking about? The kind that enhances our humanity and love for others. Failure softens our hearts and makes us sensitive to others—less judgmental and more sympathetic. If you had an unbroken string of successes, won every game you played, and turned every investment into millions of dollars, do you realize how insufferable you would be to live with? You would have an ego a mile long. But failure draws out our best traits of love and sympathy, if we learn from failure.

GETTING STARTED

Life is full of talented failures, drawing-board dreams, people with brains but no bravery, and aptitude but no action. Inertia rules so many people that they stay put forever. And yet 1 percent of acting is worth 100 percent of intent. Jesus said, "If you know these things, blessed are you if you do them," not happy are you that simply know them (John 13:17). From Genesis 1:1 forward you see God doing things: "God created." He gave you the model. Your dream doesn't begin until you start.

I often tell my congregation about things I intend to do before I know how I will do them. I tell them about illustrated sermons I will preach, ministries I will start, and goals I have. That forces me into action. I burn bridges so I can't go back on my word, and once I get started, things happen to make the vision come about. I get that power along the way that only God can give.

God has called you to dream great dreams. He has called you to be creative, like our Master. He has made you to be an explorer, an adventurer. As you begin the journey toward your dream, God will give you power along the way. With courage and God's help, you will launch out of the starting gate and into your destiny.

Study Guide Questions

1. How does your past impact your present life? Does your past ever define or limit you in a way that hinders your dream? Explain.

    _____

    _____

    _____

    _____

2. Are you ever bored or disappointed with life? Do you have a sense of unfinished business? How does this relate to your dream?

    _____

    _____

    _____

    _____

3. How has fear kept you from going after your dream? Talk about the feelings you have when you think of your dream. Do you get excited? Fearful? Tense? Happy? Anxious? Overwhelmed?

    _____

    _____

    _____

4.   Are you satisfied with your life even though your dream remains unfulfilled? What causes this attitude in you? Explain the difference between godly satisfaction and satisfaction that squelches your dreams.

_____

_____

_____

_____

5.   What does it mean to have courage? How have you displayed courage? Write down a specific incident or circumstance in which you showed courage. How will following your dream require courage from you?

_____

_____

_____

_____

6.   Think of a time when you failed on the path to your dream. What did you learn? How did that failure educate and motivate you, and how did it cultivate your character? Explain.

_____

_____

_____

_____

7. What can you do this week to progress toward your dream?

    _____

    _____

    _____

    _____

Reflections

DAY 1

Read and review the chapter material.

DAY 2

> Brothers, I do not consider myself yet to have taken hold of it. But one thing I do: Forgetting what is behind and straining toward what is ahead, I press on toward the goal to win the prize for which God has called me heavenward in Christ Jesus.
>
> —PHILIPPIANS 3:13–14, NIV

Have you ever felt dragged down by your past? Maybe you did something wrong or suffered from circumstances beyond your control. Perhaps your past is full of great victories or accomplishments that you find hard to match again.

Everybody has to deal with their past at some point, because the past can be a dream-killer. How you view your past will greatly affect how you view your future and your dream. It will influence how you speak, act, and treat other people. It will determine what you are able to accomplish for God.

As a child of God, you have been given a duty: embrace the simple truth that Christ's blood releases you entirely from the sins of the past, and you will live in victory and fulfillment. This release is complete and total; it is not conditional. God doesn't make a bargain with you that He will forgive your sins as long as you drag around the guilt for the rest of your life, telling everyone what you did and living in the shadow of that sin. No—your forgiveness is complete. You don't ever have to think about it again.

Second Corinthians 5:17 says that if we are in Christ, we are a new creation and the past is no more. By revisiting our past, we drain power from our dreams. Good things can distract us just as easily as our defeats. Perhaps you know someone who dwells on past accomplishments—a great sporting career, an outstanding academic record, a successful business endeavor—but their present and future are stalled.

The good news for every believer is that no matter how good things are now, the best is yet to come. No matter how bad things are now, the best is yet to come. No matter what has come before, you have a dream and a future, if you will take your eyes off the past and embrace your future.

1.   If there are some things—good or bad—from the past that you dwell upon, write a plan of action to forget those things and look to the future.

   _____

   _____

   _____

   _____

Ask God to help you put your past in perspective and to give you a future orientation toward your dream.

DAY 3

Then the word of the LORD came through the prophet Haggai: "Is it a time for you yourselves to be living

in your paneled houses, while this house remains a
ruin?"…"Give careful thought to your ways. Go up
into the mountains and bring down timber and build
the house, so that I may take pleasure in it and be
honored."

—Haggai 1:3–4, 7–8, niv

I considered starting a church in Los Angeles at an age when
some ministers are looking forward to retirement. The struggle
within me became intense. I would lie awake at night in a sweat
wondering what I should do. Several times I tried to abandon the
idea altogether, but a sense of unfinished business hovered over
me. I had always dreamed of having a church in Los Angeles; now
I had an opportunity. Would I let it pass by?

Like the people in Haggai's day, I had everything I needed: a
great church and family in Phoenix and a lifestyle I enjoyed. But
God had given me a dream for Los Angeles, and I couldn't let it go.
Finally, amidst all my fears, I plunged ahead and, with the help of
my son, began pastoring a small church in a very poor neighborhood. Today that church serves thirty thousand inner-city residents
a week with the gospel, food, job training, medical help, and more.
Periodicals such as the *New York Times* and the *Los Angeles Times*
have written about the church.

I'm so glad I followed that dream!

Is there unfinished business in your life that you have been
neglecting? In Haggai's day the people enjoyed the fruits of
their labor, but God's house lay in ruins. Your life may look nice
from the outside, but if you harbor a sense of unfinished business, you won't have peace. God is saying to you, "Give careful
thought to your ways. Take care of the unfinished business that
is part of your dream."

What Is Holding You Back?

It is possible that the greatest aspects of your dream remain undone. Those nagging reminders you feel may point the way to your greatest legacy. When we tackle our unfinished business, I believe we can claim the promise God gave to the people in Haggai's day who put aside their other pursuits to finish the house of God. God said:

> The glory of this present house will be greater than the glory of the former house....And in this place I will grant peace.
>
> —Haggai 2:9, NIV

1. Do you have a feeling of unfinished business? Which aspects of your dream are you not pursuing, if any? Be specific.

    _____

    _____

    _____

    _____

2. What excuses have you used to dismiss this feeling? Write them below, and then read each one aloud and cross it off, symbolizing that you won't hold that excuse any longer.

    _____

    _____

    _____

    _____

Pray that no part of your dream will go unfulfilled.

DAY 4

> Jacob said to them, "You have deprived me of my children. Joseph is no more and Simeon is no more, and now you want to take Benjamin. Everything is against me!"
>
> —GENESIS 42:36, NIV

When we were looking to buy a building for the church in Los Angeles, I felt as if everything were against me. I was certain it was God's will for us to buy a certain old waterworks building and turn it into our facility. But a company came and bought it out from under us at the last minute. I was devastated.

Then we found a bigger building for about the same price, and I became convinced it was for us. But the city council said they didn't want us to use the building for a church. I was greatly disappointed, to say the least.

In the end, we found a much bigger building that allows us to do vastly more ministry. It is better in every way. But before we found that building, I had to fight through the disappointment of losing the first two.

Have you ever felt as if everything was against you? We will all feel disappointed by people, circumstances, and even by God at times. The problem with disappointment is that it relies on our faulty interpretations and judgments of a situation. We are but jars of clay, but when we presume to know how every situation should turn out, we invite disappointment, and it can color our perspective for the rest of our lives if we are not careful.

Look at the scripture at the beginning of this entry. Jacob had "lost" his son Joseph many years earlier, and that deep disappointment poisoned his outlook. In fact, at the time he spoke these words, he was just days away from being reunited with Joseph, who had not, in fact, died. But Jacob could not see the bigger picture. He was on the verge of an amazing blessing, but he interpreted the situation according to his deep, persistent disappointment and concluded, "Everything is against me!"

Has lingering disappointment obscured your dream? If so, it's time to release disappointment and embrace the dream. You cannot hold on to both.

1. Are you disappointed with God? If so, explain why.

   _____

   _____

   _____

   _____

2. Are you disappointed with those around you? If so, journal your feelings here.

   _____

   _____

   _____

   _____

Today, force your mind to dwell more on your dream than on past disappointments. Ask God to help you drain any lingering poison of disappointment from your heart.

Day 5

[The rich man said to himself], "You have plenty of good things laid up for many years. Take life easy; eat, drink and be merry." But God said to him, "You fool! This very night your life will be demanded from you. Then who will get what you have prepared for yourself?"

—Luke 12:19–20, NIV

After every sermon I preach, I hear a voice from behind me that says, "That was pretty good, but you can do better." After every Christmas or Easter pageant at my church, that same voice says, "It was good this year, but you can do better." Every time I win a victory, big or small, this same voice reminds me, "You can do better next time."

That voice is not a person; it's godly dissatisfaction, and it's a good thing—it prods me toward my dreams. It keeps me from being satisfied.

What's wrong with satisfaction? Nothing, as long you are not *oversatisfied*. God hates it when we become too satisfied and quit pursuing our dream. It's a paradox that Jesus satisfies our souls but also creates a constant dissatisfaction within us to keep us moving forward. The prophet Amos said, "Woe to you who are complacent in Zion" (Amos 6:1, NIV). Paul said, "I do not count myself to have apprehended" (Phil. 3:13).

In America and other wealthy countries, oversatisfaction is the rule. People go to great lengths to expand their leisure time, reduce their work hours, and acquire items that help them relax: DVD players, jet skis, second homes, and third automobiles. We have made recreation a way of life.

But God said, "Woe to you who are complacent." Jesus warned that "the worries of this life and the deceitfulness of wealth" cut off the gospel's effectiveness in us, "making it unfruitful" (Matt. 13:22, NIV). Wealth quickly leads to oversatisfaction, which stops you from growing toward your dream.

1. What is your satisfaction level? Do you give too much time to idleness or recreation? Is your general feeling that your life is "good enough"? Explain.

    _____

    _____

    _____

    _____

2. How would your life be different if you lived with the same intensity of focus that Jesus did? Which habits and hobbies would you leave behind?

    _____

    _____

    _____

    _____

Ask God to give you a holy dissatisfaction that spurs you on.

Day 6

> [Saul said,] I was afraid of the people and so I gave
> in to them.
>
> —1 Samuel 15:24, niv

Has fear kept you from fighting for your dream? Let me introduce you to a man who was riddled with fear. He was Saul, the first king of Israel, and he lived one of the most tragic lives in all the Bible.

Saul had no reason to be afraid. He stood a head taller than any other Israelite. He had the anointing and blessing of God on his life. He had the support of the people.

But on the day of his coronation, Saul's fear appeared. Instead of striding forward, he hid among the baggage and had to be brought out (1 Sam. 10:22).

Later, as he prepared his army for battle, Saul disobeyed Samuel, the prophet of God, and offered a burnt offering before the appointed time. Saul was afraid that his men would scatter unless he sought the Lord's favor, and his fear drove him to do it in a way that displeased God (1 Sam. 13:7–12).

Finally, Saul failed to obey the Lord's command to kill all the livestock of his enemies after a battle. Instead, Saul gave the livestock as plunder to his soldiers. "I was afraid of the people and so I gave in to them," he admitted (1 Sam. 15:24, niv).

Eventually, Saul's fear of losing the throne drove him nearly insane, and he committed suicide on the battlefield (1 Sam. 31:4).

Fear is a sinister, dream-depriving force. Fear keeps some people from taking the first steps toward their dreams.

If you are stalled on the way to your dream, maybe you don't realize that fear is controlling you. Fear disguises itself as common sense, practicality, even wisdom; the excuses you make might be motivated by fear.

Here's how I conquer fear: instead of spending a lot of time anticipating the battle, I get to the battle quickly. I would rather be in the fight than waiting for it to start! I also remind myself that battles will come to me, even if I try to avoid them. I would rather fight battles in the direction of my dream than fight battles of someone else's choosing.

The most common command in the Bible is this: "Be not afraid!" That's good advice for you and me today.

Consider this verse:

> For God has not given us a spirit of fear, but of power
> and of love and of a sound mind.
>
> —2 TIMOTHY 1:7

1. What are you afraid of? Make a list, being as honest and complete as you can.

    _____

    _____

    _____

    _____

2. What do you think will come of your dreams if you continue to fear these things?

_____

_____

_____

_____

Confess the sin of fear to God; then put fear aside and refuse to give it a place in your mind.

DAY 7

It is good for me that I have been afflicted, that I may learn Your statutes.

—PSALM 119:71

One day I was driving by a playground when I saw a crowd of boys and girls gathered around to watch two boys fight. I jumped out of my car to stop them, and the big boy hit the smaller boy and knocked him down. The smaller boy got up and the big boy hit him again in the nose, but the small boy got up and charged the big boy again. Blood was everywhere. I finally got close enough to say, "Stop! You're going to kill that boy."

But the little boy looked at me and said, "Mister, let me go. I haven't gotten my second wind yet."

I don't know why, but something in me said, "Let him go," so I did, and he ran at the big boy, took a wild swing, hit him in the nose, and sent him away crying!

I'm against fighting, but I admire that little boy. He didn't accept failure; he learned from it until he got the upper hand.

God wants you to succeed; He wants you to grasp your dream and make it happen. But on the way, you will sometimes fail. That's how the world works—we learn more from mistakes than success. But God will educate you in the aftermath of failure. He will motivate you to try harder next time, and He will cultivate your character so you can handle success when it comes.

The psalmist said it was good for him to have been afflicted, because it forced him to learn. Success really depends on how well you handle failure. Proverbs says:

> Do not despise the chastening of the LORD, nor detest His correction; for whom the LORD loves He corrects, just as a father the son in whom he delights.
>
> —PROVERBS 3:11–12

Hebrews says:

> Now no chastening seems to be joyful for the present, but painful; nevertheless, afterward it yields the peaceable fruit of righteousness to those who have been trained by it.
>
> —HEBREWS 12:11

Failure can be such a chastening, and it can bring us closer to our dream than a constant string of success ever could.

1. Describe a recent failure you encountered on the way to your dream.

   _____

   _____

   _____

   _____

2. What did you learn from that failure?

   _____

   _____

   _____

   _____

Ask God to teach you His ways in every situation in which you find yourself.

CHAPTER THREE

Cultivate Your Dream

You've discovered your dream. You've knocked down the obstacles to pursuing it. Now you have to *grow* your dream! Every person's dream is different, but all dreams grow in the same "soil." The four main nutrients in that soil are:

1. Prayer

2. Praise

3. Bible study

4. Fellowship

Those are the basics of the Christian life, but I want to share about each one in a unique way that directly pertains to reaching your dream. At the end of this chapter, you will see these habits of dreamers in a fresh light.

Prayer

Prayer can be defined many ways, but here's a definition that works well: prayer is when you converse with God about the dreams He put in your heart. That is one of the fundamental purposes of prayer, if not *the* fundamental purpose. When we talk to God, He wants to hear about our dreams. Jesus confirmed this when He said you should pray, "Thy will be done." In other words, you should center your prayers around accomplishing the will of God. You accomplish the will of God by boldly and fearlessly following your dreams. Your prayers are the conversations you have with God about those dreams and purposes. When you pray from that perspective, your prayers become powerful as they touch the heart of God. Prayer power doesn't come from being holy, saying the right words, or praying in a certain fashion that catches God's fancy. Prayer power doesn't come after years of effort and becoming an "expert" prayer. Rather, prayer power comes from having a heart-to-heart talk with God about the plans and dreams He placed inside of you.

Without talking about your dreams, your prayers have no real content. Did you know that some prayers are weak? And that some are vain, selfish, and useless? Did you know some prayers even make God angry? He told people in the Bible, "To what purpose is the multitude of your sacrifices to Me?" (Isa. 1:11). He was essentially saying, "There is no content in your prayers. You are fasting and praying, but I am not paying any attention to you because your prayers lack purpose."

Dreamless prayer is impotent prayer. God dislikes aimless chatter just as much as we do. You could pray twelve hours a day, but if there were no purpose or point to it, it wouldn't have any effect. It would be empty talk. God doesn't fellowship with nothingness. He condemned people in the Bible for repetitious prayer, for praying without purpose and repeating the same words over and over. You have probably had hallway conversations with a co-worker where you stopped and chatted for a moment. Usually those conversations go for a minute or two, and unless it goes somewhere, you lose interest. To continue would be vain and fruitless. The Bible says many times to avoid worldly and empty chatter (1 Tim. 5:13). We shouldn't let our tongues wag on and on, or our careless words will lead to further ungodliness (v. 15). You can actually provoke people to ungodliness by empty words, and their talk "will spread like gangrene" (2 Tim. 2:17, NIV).

The same principle governs prayer. Aimless chatter can fill our heads with purposeless thoughts and anxieties. But when our prayers spring from our passionate desire to fulfill our dreams, prayer becomes powerful. That's when we touch the heart of God with requests, observations, and meditations on the dreams He put inside of us. Prayer comes to life when our dreams intersect with God's will, when we run to Him with ideas, questions, and requests about our purpose on earth. God told the people through the prophet Isaiah, "Look to the rock from which you were hewn.... Look to Abraham your father" (Isa. 51:1–2). The place of power in prayer—the place where God listens and communes with us—is directly related to our dreams. He was pointing them back to their purpose. Then, the Lord said, He would "comfort all her waste places; He will make her wilderness like Eden, and her desert like the garden of the LORD" (v. 3).

If you have never had a healthy prayer time with God, perhaps it's because you have never talked to Him about your dreams. Prayer is not, "Holy God, if thou wouldst listen to Your servant, a sinner, while I lay my requests before Thee." It's, "God, I want to get together and visit with You awhile. Here are the thoughts that are on my heart. Here's what I've been thinking of doing. What do You think?" Prayer is being with God like two best friends. Once your life is oriented toward pursuing your dreams with all your heart, prayer opens up and becomes the place where you can discuss with God whatever you want to discuss. Your heart and His will be in constant accord, and that friendship will nurture your dreams and your very soul.

For years I have prayed every morning on the mountainside near our church. I go there early with my Bible and a big cup of Starbucks coffee, and I approach prayer as if I'm getting to spend time with my best friend in the whole world. What do you do when you spend time with your best friend? You do whatever you want! Sometimes I tell Him my problems, and I weep and say, "God, I need Your help." At other times I share my joys, and I rejoice, laugh, praise, and shout. Other times I don't feel like talking, so I just listen. I have worn a path pacing back and forth on that ledge over the years. Everyone should have a place they can go and be with God. I pace on that mountainside. You might meet with God in your car, closet, backyard, or in the woods.

As you grow in God and in the direction of your dreams, all the extraneous "filler" will disappear from your prayers. You will find He is interested in anything you are sincerely interested in. He wants to get to know you; He wants your relationship to develop as you fulfill the goals He put in your heart. He will become your best friend.

And remember this fundamental fact regarding prayer: God exalts the humble but resists the proud.

That puts God within reach of any one of us. Lift up Jesus, and He will lift you up. Dream His dreams, and He will fill your life with understanding and power. He doesn't exalt the intelligent and the proper, but the humble. Come into His presence just as you are and let your conversations with Him be filled with the plan and purpose for which you were made.

PERFECTED PRAISE

Another important habit for a dreamer is praise. Because of our many, varied backgrounds, it's easy for that word to be colored in many different ways. Does it mean quietly reverencing God? Falling on your knees? Singing loud? Singing quietly? Closing your eyes? Or opening them and gazing toward heaven? Does it mean lifting your hands or folding them?

I believe God is less concerned with the "how" of praise than He is with the heart of praise. One peculiar Bible passage gives us a key to this subject. It says:

> Out of the mouth of babes and nursing infants You
> have perfected praise.
>
> —MATTHEW 21:16

Strangely, Jesus said praise is perfected by little children. The word *perfect* in this passage means "matured," meaning that the most mature praise on the planet comes from a little child. How can that be? Jesus was saying that perfect praise is first-time praise. It springs from the same fresh realization and wonder we feel upon experiencing something for the first time. For example, you may have seen a little baby at the moment he first discovered his hand. He held it up and turned it around, examining it in awe. You probably stared eagerly at your child's face when he or she first ate watermelon or other foods. You might have even videotaped it. That moment of discovery and wonder brings something up within the human soul: that something is *praise*.

The greatest secret I have ever discovered in my pursuit for perfect praise is this: approach everything you do as if it were the first time, and let that awe and eagerness and wonder swell within you, becoming praise to God. For example, every time I get into my car, I feel like it's the first time. Why? Because I remember the first vehicle I ever had, a '55 Jeep station wagon I nicknamed "She Needs" because "she needed" cans and cans of oil, gas, and paint. But I loved that car. I was so proud of it. Just thinking about it brings back the perfected praise I felt when I first turned that key in the ignition.

Then I remember my first new car, a '61 peach and white Plymouth with fender skirts, foxtails, and reflectors on the mud flaps. It was a beauty. When I think of it, I remember that perfected praise of having my first new car. I feel the same thrill from that moment, and my heart rejoices in God and in that experience.

Every time I get on an airplane to fly somewhere, I get excited. I never lose the joy of flying. My wife has heard me say again and again, "I just love to fly." Every time is just like the first time.

Every time I go overseas, it's as if I've never been there before. Everything looks exotic and new, and my heart fills with praise for God, because it feels like a brand-new experience.

Every time I stay in a motel, I get excited to be there, just like when I was a kid.

Every vacation I take is like the first one I took to Mexico City, driving all the way from Kansas City. I remember sharing our *dulces* (candies) with the kids there, sometimes throwing candy out the windows all along the highway. I relive that thrill every time I go on vacation, even now.

I have lived in Phoenix for more than twenty-five years, but I still can't get enough of the mountains in our city. I point them out all the time to my staff and my family, and sometimes they laugh at me because I never get tired of the mountains. When I was in Davenport, Iowa, I used to do the same with the river that ran through town. It always looked new and different to me.

Whenever I open the Bible, I remember when it first came alive to me. I remember that moment as a little boy when I first truly understood, deep in my young soul, that Jesus loved me as if I were the only person on Planet Earth. That feeling explodes in me every day as if it were happening for the first time.

I remember the first time I discovered that I could communicate with God in prayer, and that His presence would be with me wherever I went. I remember when the Holy Spirit became a person to me instead of an experience or some distant, mysterious being.

I have first-time experiences every day of my life. It's called perfected praise, having the excitement of your first love. The longer you serve God, the better it can get. Every day with Jesus is sweeter than the day before. You can go through life jaded and world-weary, and everything will seem old, tired, and worn. Or you can go through life with excitement, wonder, and joy as if experiencing every meal, every sunrise, every kiss for the first time. That, the Bible says, is perfected praise. It causes songs and words of praise and worship to overflow from your heart and spring from your lips. You will sing and speak praises to God almost continually when you realize His goodness over and over again, like a little child. You will praise Him when you wake up, as you go to work, when you come home. You will praise Him when you are full of physical energy and when you are very tired. You will enjoy each mood, each circumstance, each facet of life because of its unique pleasure and challenge. Praise is much more than fifteen minutes of music on Sunday morning; praise is a lifestyle that propels us forward in our dreams.

When we practice perfected praise, we keep God in mind all the time. Instead of feeling as if we are pursuing our dream alone, we recognize again and again that it was His dream for us to begin with, and He is helping us accomplish it. When praise saturates your soul, it energizes you for whatever task you face. Your dream comes alive just as it did the first time you realized that God has a plan for you. His desires for you are good, and He wants to give you the desires of your heart. Nothing promotes your dream like perfected praise, because it keeps you close to that original flame. When you are able to praise God in every-thing, you remind yourself how good He is to you and that He is working with you so you will achieve everything He has put in your heart.

TRANSFORMED AND RENEWED

The third habit of dreamers is to let God's truths shape their thoughts and ideas rather than allowing the influences around you to shape them. Each of us comes to this present moment with a set of opinions, outlooks, and perspectives that were formed by countless factors: our upbringing, family, school experience, jobs, and so on. As we go through life, we may fit ourselves to many forms. Some people find a form they like and stay in it for the rest of their lives. Perhaps it was the form they received as children, as college students, or in a certain occupation. The question is not will your mind be formed, but what will form it?

Form determines the shape of something. It's a pattern, like when you pour concrete into a formboard or pour gelatin into a mold. The Bible says, "Be transformed by the renewing of your mind" (Rom. 12:2). This means you should let the Bible determine the "shape" of your thought life. To *transform* means to go beyond the set form, to change in structure and nature. Perhaps you have a cup of coffee or some other drink nearby. The liquid of that drink is conformed to the shape of the cup it is in. Nothing will change the shape as long as it is in that cup. You can bless it and turn it into holy water or add sugar or cream to it, but the shape of that liquid will remain stubbornly the same. To transform it, you must remove it from the cup that is forming it.

That's how our minds operate. To transform them, they must be removed from the conforming influence around us and put into a form whose dimensions are specified by the Word of God. When we let the Bible transform our minds, we release our dreams from the forms that have held them back. It's like Gulliver in the book *Gulliver's Travels* when he is held down by the Lilliputians and their hundreds of tiny ropes. Those ropes are like the lies and half-truths we believed before we came to know Christ. The Word of God breaks those ropes one by one every time you read and meditate on it. The Word of God breaks old forms that tie up your dreams, and it releases your potential at greater levels than you have known in the past. Dreams can only flourish in a mind that is formed by the eternal Word of God.

I grew up with a dad who was a pastor. You would think that everybody in the church was nice and friendly, but the people in our church were almost entirely negative. They said we couldn't play sports because it wasn't spiritual. They argued over the lessons in Sunday school and challenged the preacher after every sermon. My dad was formed by that environment, and he was not an affectionate or outwardly loving man. But one day he had a realization that his form was wrong, and he decided he wasn't going to be that way anymore. From that point on, he grew into the most loving, affectionate man I ever knew. He changed my life and many others because he broke the form that had been handed to him. He allowed God's Word to transform his mind.

Paul said, "If anyone is in Christ, he is a new creation; old things have passed away; behold, all things have become new" (2 Cor. 5:17). Everyone who goes to church or a home gathering brings with them their learned doctrine. Some come from a Catholic, Baptist, Mormon, Pentecostal, or atheist background. But are we being transformed by the Word rather than our traditions?

Jesus said of the Pharisees, "You have made the commandment of God of no effect by your tradition" (Matt. 15:6). If you want to reach your dreams, then let those traditions fall away. Read the Bible as much as you reasonably can to allow the old form to come off and the new, dream-empowering form to transform your mind.

DREAMING TOGETHER

The last important habit of dreamers is fellowship. Everybody needs a place where they can go and share their dreams and plans with people who won't laugh or make fun of them. Fellowship is built on encouragement. It should strengthen you, build you up, and help you to see your life and dreams more clearly.

When small groups have times of fellowship and meeting each others' needs, it should be in an atmosphere of complete

encouragement. Some people think they have the gift of construc-
tive criticism, but I rarely hear criticism that builds someone up.
Rather, the way to encourage people to their highest potential
is by bragging on them. Tell them how great they are. Point out
their strengths. Be amazed by their gifts. People should leave with
a spark of joy in their hearts. They should find the support they
need to continue on toward their dream.

I have noticed a wicked tendency in my own life sometimes.
When I know what somebody wants, I withhold it from them.
For example, someone walks into the room wearing a brand-
new outfit, and I say to myself, *She wants me to say how nice
her dress is, but I'm not going to.* Or an elderly person says,
"Nobody needs me any more. I'm not loved by anyone," and I
think, *I wish he'd quit whining.* Why not give them what they
want? Give people the compliments they are asking for. Tell the
lady, "Wow! What a great outfit." Tell the old person, "I need
you, and I don't know what I'd do without you." Give people
what they need instead of dismissing them as gripers. Let God
do the tearing down if it's needed. Let us be the ones to build
them up.

Fellowship should also have a well-defined purpose.
Relationship without purpose is not enough. Fellowship alone,
for its own sake, will not produce good fruit. Home meetings,
even those centered around Bible study, can actually become
harmful if they wander from their purpose. The people might
get together and have a marvelous time studying the Word.
Then they might linger over dessert and coffee, chatting about
the church, and soon they are criticizing each other, the pastor,
the nursery workers, and other church leaders. Proper fellowship is powerful; improper fellowship can be destructive, even
to those involved.

I believe all small groups should exist to introduce people to Christ. At my church in Phoenix we have more than two hundred ministries operating in the church, and each functions as a small group while at the same time staying focused on a ministry purpose. Some ministries reach out to unwed mothers, bikers, street children, or athletes. But each has a purpose when the group comes together. Fellowship happens in the context of ministry. When your focus is on outreach, it takes your mind off of yourself and puts it onto others.

The small groups that are meeting to read this book should have a goal of bringing new people every week. That should be your ambition. You will be amazed what it does to the life of the group and the church to have new believers among you. It will revolutionize you as a person. It will refresh you, change you, and open your mind to the many ways God works. You will grow in God faster than ever because you are partnering with Him in work that's close to His heart.

The fellowship groups should also have time limits, so people don't hang around talking forever. Proverbs 10:19 says, "In the multitude of words sin is not lacking," and Paul reminds us, "Whatever things are true…just…pure…lovely…meditate on these things" (Phil. 4:8). It's possible to leave a Bible study meeting more stressed and down in the dumps than when you came because the conversation got off track and became unhealthy, even if what was discussed was true and had the flavor of spirituality.

But with a clear purpose, defined goals, and time limits, a small group can have an amazing impact. If your small group is to continue beyond the seven weeks in this study, make sure it has a clearly defined and measurable ministry purpose. That purpose may be to function as an engine of evangelism, pulling people into the kingdom of God, getting them plugged in to the life of the church, and inspiring them to dream with God. Or your small group should release its members to join existing ministries of the church—or start new ones—and enjoy fellowship within the context of that ministry.

The reason it's important to cultivate your dream with these four habits is because no dream will flourish in the wrong soil. You could choose to ignore these habits, but I can guarantee that your dream would stall, the excitement would go out of it, and you would lose that strong connection you feel to your destiny. Instead, cultivate a life of:

1. Prayer

2. Perfected praise

3. Bible reading

4. Fellowship

Your dream will grow steady and strong!

Study Guide Questions

1. What is prayer to you? What do you do when you pray? What words do you say or songs do you sing? Do you pray for an hour straight or for a few minutes here and there? Do you talk a lot, or do you listen? Are you formal or informal with God?

    _____

    _____

    _____

    _____

2. How would you like your prayer life to change? What can you do to change it?

    _____

    _____

    _____

    _____

3. What does "perfected praise" mean to you?

    _____

    _____

    _____

    _____

4.   Choose the words below that describe your usual frame of mind:

Jaded   World-weary
Bored   Excited
Innocent   Fresh
Energized   "Been there, done that"

What steps can you take to cultivate an attitude of perfected praise in the coming days?

_____

_____

_____

_____

5.   How often do you read the Bible? What results do you see in yourself when your mind is being renewed and transformed by God's Word? Have you ever fallen into a place of stagnation? How did you know?

_____

_____

_____

_____

6. What kind of fellowship do you have with other believers? Do you have rich friendships with Christians that go back years, or do you have only "foyer" relationships? What kind of fellowship would you like to have with other Christians? What social settings do you enjoy? What are you looking for in relationships?

_____

_____

_____

_____

Reflections

Day 1

Read and review the chapter material.

Day 2

> And when you pray, do not keep on babbling like
> pagans, for they think they will be heard because
> of their many words. Do not be like them, for your
> Father knows what you need before you ask him.
>
> —Matthew 6:7–8, niv

People pray differently. I watched the president's inauguration some years back, and several ministers prayed during the ceremony. Billy Graham prayed a warm, passionate prayer as if God were standing right in front of him. Many hearts were stirred. But his prayer was not typical. Most of the ministers stepped to the podium and pulled out a long, written prayer and read it as if they were reciting from the phone book. As I watched, I wondered, *Is that how they talk to God in private?*

Each of us has a different prayer routine. Each of us talks to God in different ways and in different postures. Some people stand, some kneel, some walk around, and others lie on their face. It's good to have freedom in prayer, but Jesus expressly told us *not* to pray in a certain way: He told us not to babble. To babble is to talk excessively, idly, or insincerely. When you say things over and over thinking it will gain favor or acceptance from God, you treat God not as a partner but as a dispensing machine. Also, when you babble, it means you have lost sight of your dream and are wandering all over the place in your mind.

God ultimately doesn't want our words; He wants our hearts. The Bible says, "Man looks at the outward appearance, but the LORD looks at the heart" (1 Sam. 16:7).

What does God hear when you pray? Does He see a heart at rest in Him? Jesus said our Father already knows what we need before we ask Him. Our prayers should be meaningful and from the heart, and we should measure our words by quality, not quantity.

1. What do you do during your prayer routine? Write down how you approach prayer time.

_____

_____

_____

_____

2. Take note of what you wrote above. How can you improve the quality of your prayers? What can you do to change your prayer life so that it becomes your time with God rather than a tradition?

_____

_____

_____

_____

Ask God to help you develop a prayer life pleasing to Him.

DAY 3

> Then the man and his wife heard the sound of the
> LORD God as he was walking in the garden in the cool
> of the day.
>
> —GENESIS 3:8, NIV

I love being with my children so much that every minute to me is like gold. They are all grown up now, but sometimes I'll be with one of them for an evening, and as the night goes on I try to stretch out the time and get them to stay because I want to talk with them. I get such pleasure from it.

God created you and me to have that kind of relationship with Him. He created a beautiful place called the Garden of Eden, where He wanted to spend time with men and women, you and me. He didn't even wait for Adam or Eve to find Him. He personally went to where they were, seeking fellowship.

What did Adam, Eve, and God talk about in those days before sin? The Lord came to them "in the cool of the day," after their work was completed. I believe that hints to us that Adam and Eve talked with Him about their work, their dreams, what they accomplished that day, and what their plans were for the earth that God had given them. Fellowship was about sharing dreams, resting, and enjoying one another.

Man no longer lives in that perfect garden, but that intimate place with God is still available to us. In fact, we must journey to that place often if our dream is to retain its power. That place is called prayer. The Bible tells us that the Lord "knew [Moses] face to face" (Deut. 34:10).

They had a friendship and partnership, such that Moses spoke with God openly, honestly, and often. That is a model for our relationship with God. We must learn to walk and talk with Him, speaking with Him as with a friend. Paul wrote:

> But we all, with unveiled face, beholding as in a mirror the glory of the Lord, are being transformed into the same image from glory to glory.
>
> —2 CORINTHIANS 3:18

He was saying that through open fellowship with God, we become more like Him. Our dreams thrive. That, ultimately, is one of the main purposes of prayer.

1. How would you characterize your relationship with God? Use key words like *close, distant, loving,* or *formal.*

    _____

    _____

    _____

    _____

2. Have you ever spoken to God as to a friend? Did you feel this was irreverent or pleasing to Him?

    _____

    _____

    _____

    _____

3. Imagine yourself walking and talking with God. What would you say to God if He invited you to take a stroll with Him?

_____

_____

_____

_____

Pray that you would have the kind of intimate relationship with God He desires to have with you.

DAY 4

Out of the mouth of babes and sucklings thou hast perfected praise.

—MATTHEW 21:16, KJV

Once I asked a well-known minister who had been saved from a life of gangs and drugs, "You've given your testimony thousands of times. How do you still tell it like it's fresh?"

He said, "Every time I tell it, I go back and remember how it was when I was a little drug-addicted boy. I remember being in that violent gang and how there was no hope for me until Jesus came into my life and saved me. I live it all over again every time I tell it."

That is a remarkable statement, yet it is the key to perfecting our praise. Each time this man spoke of his testimony, he revisited that first-time experience in his heart. It became like a touchstone to which he could return, renewing the gratitude and praise he felt for being rescued from a terrible life. He never tells his testimony for the thousandth—or two thousandth—time. For him, it is always the first time.

I made up my mind years ago that I would have first-time experiences every day of my life, from the moment I get up until the moment I go to bed. I wouldn't get accustomed to anything or bored with anything, because if life became one long "been there, done that," it would sap the praise right out of my heart.

Perfected praise will make you mature by making you child-like! Jesus said the most mature praise comes from first-timers—children, the newly saved. Those who "grow" in the Lord and turn praise into a bland routine have slipped into immaturity and imperfect praise.

But those who walk with God and experience everything in life as for the first time constantly rediscover the fountain of praise that wells up in renewed gratitude for God's goodness.

1.   Revisit the moment you accepted Christ into your heart.

     a.   Describe your Christian walk and thought life during those early days.

     _____

     _____

     _____

     _____

b. Describe your Christian walk and thought life as it is today.

_____

_____

_____

_____

c. If life has become a bland routine for you, what are some steps you can take to regain childlike faith and perfected praise?

_____

_____

_____

_____

Pray that God would teach you perfected praise by giving you a sense of wonder in all you do.

DAY 5

> Then the brethren immediately sent Paul and Silas away by night to Berea. When they arrived, they went into the synagogue of the Jews. These were more fair-minded than those in Thessalonica, in that they received the word with all readiness, and searched the Scriptures daily to find out whether these things were so. Therefore many of them believed.
>
> —ACTS 17:10–12

The difference why some people read the Bible and get so much out of it, and others read it and don't seem to improve their lives at all, is in how they approach it and what it does to their heart.

The Berean Jews searched the Scriptures fair-mindedly, ready to hear what God had to say to them about the Messiah. They grasped that the point of reading God's Word is not simply to gain knowledge or to have a convincing theology, but to be reintroduced daily to God in a way you have not yet fully known.

Other Jews were not so fair-minded. The Pharisees were more committed to their tradition than to God, and so the Scriptures became dead to them. It could not lead them to Jesus. They would not hear God speaking to them through the pages of Scripture. Jesus told them they did not have the love of God in their hearts. (See John 5:39–42.)

How should we approach the Bible? With love and openness toward God. If we love other things more than we love Him, our vision will be clouded and warped, and we might use the Bible to justify all kinds of things God never intended. Rather, we should be ready to learn new things about Him. Through the

Bible He will reveal Himself to us every day, and He will speak to us about who He is and who we are in Him.

1. When you read the Bible, have there ever been times when you felt the Word was falling on the hardened soil of your heart? Can you give reasons why?

_____

_____

_____

_____

2. When was the Bible most alive to you?

_____

_____

_____

3. Have you ever felt so bound by tradition that you were unable to learn more about God? Were these traditions imposed on you, or did you impose them on yourself? Explain.

_____

_____

_____

_____

Pray that the Bible will lead you closer to God, breaking traditions that bind you.

DAY 6

> Do not conform any longer to the pattern of this world, but be transformed by the renewing of your mind. Then you will be able to test and approve what God's will is—his good, pleasing and perfect will.
>
> —ROMANS 12:2, NIV

When I was a boy, I knew without a doubt that my father was a rich man. We lived in Armordale, the best area of Kansas City for building a great church. Our neighborhood was a place where people seized opportunities, followed great dreams, and built great businesses. I had every reason to expect that I would succeed in life.

That was my reality until the day I spoke at a church growth conference and a man introduced me by saying, "My father pastored in Armordale, where Tommy Barnett's father pastored, and I can tell you, Tommy Barnett was not born with a silver spoon in his mouth. Armordale was the worst part of the city. It's where all the poor people lived, and the Barnett house was a hundred yards from the railroad tracks."

My jaw nearly dropped as he described it, and I realized he was right. My neighborhood was the kind of place people wanted to flee. It was bound by poverty and negative thinking. My family had been poor, too. But I had never seen it that way.

Though I grew up in Armordale, I never had an Armordale mentality. My parents always told me, "You can do anything you want. You could be a professional ballplayer or a movie star." They created great vistas in my mind with their words.

God gives us the same opportunity to shape our minds with His Word. In fact, His dreams for us are much greater than even what my parents dreamed for me. To God, we are the righteousness of Christ, priests to our God, the apple of His eye.

When you read the Bible and dream with God, you begin to share His perspective. You may live in your own "Armordale," but your dreams can lead you wherever you want to go, if you let God transform your mind and your dreams.

1. Whose words and which circumstances shaped your outlook on life?

    _____

    _____

    _____

    _____

2. If you are to reach your dreams, which of those old forms need to be broken? Be specific.

    _____

    _____

    _____

    _____

Pray that your mind would be shaped solely by the living Word of God.

DAY 7

> Let us not give up meeting together, as some are in the
> habit of doing, but let us encourage one another—and
> all the more as you see the Day approaching.
>
> —HEBREWS 10:25, NIV

My church and I have been through more great experiences together than most people could imagine. More victories, more mountaintop moments, more new frontiers, and more rough times, too. But through it all we have encouraged each other and spurred each other on to our dreams. Without the deep, godly fellowship we have enjoyed, we would not have reached so many of our dreams as a church body and as individuals.

The purpose of fellowship is so that we might encourage one another to pursue our dreams. It is an opportunity to build each other up and provide the support needed to carry on. Fellowship in a church, in particular small groups such as the one you are attending weekly, is vital to introducing people to Christ. The interest or ministry purpose initially draws likeminded people together, but the focus is to lift up Jesus. It's important to have a time limit, too, on fellowship meetings. If the afterglow of these meetings becomes the main event of getting together, then it can have a negative spiritual impact on you.

The Bible says we are members of one another (Rom. 12). There is power in celebrating together, bearing one another's burdens, meeting each other's needs, and encouraging each other. To fully live, each of us must encourage others and be encouraged by others. Only then will we have the strength and energy we need to reach our dreams.

1.   Have you ever experienced "bad" fellowship, where negativity, griping, or gossiping prevailed? In your opinion, what breeds such attitudes? How do you turn them around? Explain.

   _____

   _____

   _____

   _____

2.   What are some key characteristics of healthy fellowship? Make a list.

   _____

   _____

   _____

   _____

Ask God to pervade the fellowship you have with other believers. If need be, ask Him to change atmospheres where you work, live, or attend church so that healthy fellowship will prevail.

CHAPTER FOUR

Multiply Your Dream

*B*y now you should have a good idea what your dream is. You should have overcome what was keeping you in the starting gate. You should be cultivating the dream with prayer, perfected praise, Bible study, and fellowship with other believers.

Now we will discuss something I consider critical to the success of any dream. It may seem unusual, even backwards, but I assure you that no dream that is God's dream will come to pass without this key element.

That element is multiplication.

You see, it is not enough to cultivate your dream, because if your dreaming becomes self-focused and introspective, it will die. It is not enough to work hard for a personal goal, although there is much good in that. God requires of every dreamer that we multiply our dreams by lavishly giving away our resources and serving others. Sound backwards? Therein lies the secret.

Most people think the way to win a battle or accomplish a goal is by marshalling all they have, squeezing out every last resource of time and money, and launching an offensive. That is true, in part. But if we hoard everything for ourselves, we are going against one of God's fundamental principles, which is this: if you want something, give it away.

In other words, if you want your dream to come true, be generous with the very resources that will help it come true. If you want your dream to become reality, help other people reach their dreams first. Give your time and money. Serve others with enthusiasm. Evangelize and bring others to Christ. When God sees that generosity of heart, He won't be able to resist pouring new blessings and resources upon you. Jesus said:

> Give, and it will be given to you: good measure, pressed down, shaken together, and running over.
>
> —LUKE 6:38

Proverbs 11:24 says:

> There is one who scatters, yet increases more; and there is one who withholds more than is right, but it leads to poverty. The generous soul will be made rich, and he who waters will also be watered himself.

For dreamers, generosity is not an option; it's a way of life. It's the only path to fulfilling your dream and multiplying the dreams of others. Without generosity, you severely limit what God is able to do through you and in you. The Bible commands us to be generous with God and with others and to serve them. Jesus said:

> But whoever desires to become great among you shall
> be your servant.
>
> —MARK 10:43

Jesus did that very thing, "taking the form of a bondservant" (Phil. 2:7). He came to serve, and He accomplished the greatest dream this world has ever known. We also must live to serve. We must embark on the generous lifestyle.

God is so generous! He doesn't just do generous things; generosity defines Him. Psalm 51:12 says, "Uphold me by Your generous Spirit."

One of the most well-known verses in the Bible says, "For God so loved the world that He *gave*…" (John 3:16). God demonstrated that when you give, you gain much more in return. He gave His Son and gained the hearts of all who would believe in Him. Similarly, we gain every time we give something away.

When you give energy, you gain energy. Every person knows that when you do nothing all day, you feel more tired than if you had worked. But when you work, you mysteriously have more energy than if you hadn't given that energy away.

When you give strength by working out your muscles, you gain more muscle.

When you give time, somehow you seem to have more time, or you use your time better.

When you give knowledge away, God seems to sharpen your mind with new knowledge and wisdom.

When you give away your best ideas, more ideas flood your mind.

Why does this principle work? Because when you give what you have, you are declaring that God is the supplier of every resource needed to fulfill your dream. Indeed, by giving we acknowledge that He gave us every minute of life and breath; He gave us the energy and strength to work, the mind to have ideas, and the heart to love. Everything we have comes from Him, and the only way to make your dreams come true is by recognizing it and declaring with your actions: "I will give because my supply is unlimited!"

That is the attitude God blesses. The key to reaching your dreams is emptying yourself. Full vessels can't be filled. A closed hand can't receive anything. Instead of hoarding your hours, you should give generous service to others. Instead of being tight-fisted with your money, you should hunt down opportunities to write a check to a person or ministry that needs it. That signals to God that you put your dream in His hands and that you know you can't fulfill it in your own time and with your own resources.

Generosity is not a mad moment where you lose your senses and write a big check or give something precious away. Generosity is a stance, a posture, a way of living. And when generosity is your stance, everything becomes a chance to be generous. A birthday rolls around, and you feel like giving a big gift; at the restaurant you want to leave a significant tip for the waiter; when you drive, you let other people get in front of you; when you see someone panhandling, you want to lessen their suffering.

Generosity will revolutionize your outlook on life, your finances, and your attitude toward others. If you are skeptical, try it for a month or two. Give whenever you want to; go out of your way to pay for things, make donations, and be charitable. Be magnanimous with your family, friends, and co-workers. Devise generous plans (Isa. 32:8) for people, starting with your family and then moving on to people you don't even know who could use your generosity. Write a check to that local charity or ministry you have heard good things about; bring a bag of groceries to the family down the street.

You will find yourself growing happier by the day, because the only way to be happy is by bringing happiness to others. God designed humans to be happy only when they are giving themselves away. When you focus on your own pleasure, you quickly hit a ceiling where you can't take in anymore. But when you give pleasure, the joy never runs out. You can give and give and give, and it always multiplies joy both for you and for the one who receives it.

One of the themes of my ministry is, "Find a hurt and heal it. Find a need and fill it." Look around for needs, and rejoice when you find them. You will find supernatural supply replenishing your time, your ideas, your finances, and your joy. God will add high-octane fuel to your dream tank, and you will go further and faster than you thought possible. I believe some people never reach their dreams because they are not generous with others. In God's economy, the surest way to limit your success is to hold tightly to what you have. In His economy, you only get more by giving more.

Perhaps you are already generous. But there is always another level. You cannot outgive God, but it is fun once you begin to try. Take your generosity up a notch. Give more than you usually do, and see what happens. Don't split the meal check with your co-workers; pay for it all now and then. Test the boundaries of His supply. He said in Malachi:

And try Me now in this...if I will not open for you the
windows of heaven.

—MALACHI 3:10

Once you learn the joy of serving others, you won't want to
live any other way. Generous living becomes a breeze. It enlarges
your spirit, and it empowers and multiplies other people's
dreams. You have the privilege of becoming God's channel of
supply for other people.

Think about it: When you give money to help hungry people,
you literally give life to those people. They are in a better position
to discover and fulfill the dream God put within them. When you
give money to a scholarship fund, you make a student's dream
possible. When you volunteer at a school or Sunday school, you
leave a lasting memory in the minds of those children.

And sometimes as you are giving your "dream" away, you
will find your dream coming to pass. It's a biblical pattern that
sometimes you need to support someone else's dream before
your dream bears fruit. By giving your time and energy to
them, you give God an opportunity to build character in you
so that one day your dream will explode into being. A good
example of this is Joseph from the Book of Genesis.

Joseph was stuck in a prison for years, unable to follow his
own dream. While there, he worked diligently to make the prison
run well. He supported Pharaoh's dream with his best ideas and
energy. Then one day Joseph interpreted a dream for a fellow
inmate, a butler who went on to be released and given a position
of power. Later that butler remembered Joseph, and soon Joseph
became the second-in-command in Egypt.

If that seems like a roundabout way to get your dream fulfilled,
it is. But that's how God often works. While you are trying to get

your dream established, help someone else fulfill his dream, either by serving him directly or being generous. Join a ministry or business; give your time and energy to someone else. Learn skills that put you closer to reaching your dream. Serve as best you can. Sometimes you will get involved in a dream that is much bigger than yours, and it will have a draft effect. You will be pulled along. That happens all the time at my church. People come on staff and help build my dream, and along the way God gives them ideas and power to fulfill their dream.

LOVE

You can give your time, your money, your encouragement, your advice and wisdom, or anything else of value that you possess. But the single greatest way to multiply people's dreams is by giving away love.

Love is like the other resources God gives us: it is limitless. Because you are a follower of Christ, Love Himself lives inside of you. That Love never ends. The poet Robert Browning called it "imprisoned splendor." He wrote not of how to get love into us, but how to get the imprisoned love within us to flow to others! As a believer, all the love you need is already inside of you. If you find a way to release that splendor, it will come back multiplied. Solomon said:

> Cast your bread upon the waters, for you will find it
> after many days.
>
> —ECCLESIASTES 11:1

Love as if your love is unlimited, and you will find it is. We shouldn't store love up. It is not for a rainy day. It is a checking account, not a savings account. Tell people how great they are. Exaggerate a little so they have something to live up to. The truth is, it's not good enough to feel love for someone. You have to show them and tell them. Love without expression is useless. When was the last time you told someone you loved and appreciated him or her? Are you giving your love away or holding on to it? Are you creating outlets for the "imprisoned splendor" to flow? You may be poor in every other area of life, but you are extremely wealthy in love. You have an infinite amount inside of you. Spend it!

Some of us fear loving because we think it won't mean much to the person to whom we give it. But is that really true? Every time someone expresses love to me, I just melt. I feel so good. I go home encouraged, bucked up, and lighter in my soul. Why wouldn't it do the same to others? Some of us feel awkward expressing love, but there is no wrong way to go about it. People read your heart and know. One time a high school boy made an appointment to see me, and I asked what he had come to see me about. He started to stammer and turn red, but he clearly wanted to say something that was on his heart. After a few painful minutes of not even completing a sentence, he blurted out, "Pastor, I love you!" Then he got up and bolted from my office! I ran after him and asked if he'd ever told someone he loved them, and he hadn't. But he had taken a risk and been generous with his love. It made me feel great, but I bet it made him feel greater.

Be generous with love. God wants to love people, but He can only express it through us. I am amazed to say that the more love I give away, the more I get in return. When I was young, I loved less, but I used it and it expanded. God gave me deeper love as long as I kept using it. The truth is, none of us have love—we use love. And God will give you as much love as you will use.

The other aspect of multiplying your dream is to introduce people to Jesus. This is the greatest and most God-pleasing form of multiplication in the entire created world. God is a God of multiplication and expansion. The very universe, we are told, is expanding at an incredible rate. From the very beginning of the earth, God displayed His love of seeing things multiply and bear fruit. He told Adam and Eve to "be fruitful and multiply; fill the earth and subdue it" (Gen. 1:28). God told Abraham, "I will make you a great nation...Your descendants [will be] as the sand which is on the seashore" (Gen. 12:2; 22:17). Jesus told the disciples, "Go and make disciples of all nations" (Matt. 28:19, NIV).

Those are statements of multiplication. Just as God wants your dreams and abilities to multiply and bear greater and greater fruit, He wants the reach of His love and goodness to spread throughout the world. When you meet Jesus, you come into the realm of His mercy, goodness, and infinite love. The Bible calls this His "kingdom." In that kingdom are the infinite resources needed to sustain you, build your character, and fulfill your dream. Everything you ever need in life is found in God's realm of supply, and as a Christian, you have access to it, as the Bible says:

> If you ask anything in My name, I will do it.
>
> —JOHN 14:14

Not only that, but you become friends with the Creator of the universe! Jesus said:

> No longer do I call you servants...but I have called you friends.
>
> —JOHN 15:15

105

As a believer, you have what other people want and need; you hold the key to introduce them to their dreams, because without Jesus, no dream makes sense. One of our long-term goals as individuals, small groups, and churches should be to let other people see the love of God at work in us and invite them into relationship with Him. Some people will want that relationship instantly; others will hang around for a while before making a decision. Our responsibility is simply to love them, be with them, and let Jesus be who He is through us.

Of the things I'm most excited about in these small groups is that they will become communities where nonbelievers and believers mix, and people see the qualities of Jesus on display in the fellowship of believers. I imagine people stepping through the door into a small group meeting and feeling engulfed by love and acceptance. I picture them finding safe haven from the cold, lonely world. I picture groups becoming engines of life and transformation, bringing others into that realm of God's goodness and mercy, adding people to the church, and energizing it continually.

I have long taught that a pastor's job is not soul-winning; that's the people's job. The function of a pastor is to strengthen and edify the members of a church, though a pastor should also be a soulwinner simply because he or she is a Christian. We shouldn't expect people to come to know Jesus inside a church building. That's not where most of the life of a church takes place; rather, it's where people receive instruction and guidance in the Word. But most of the influence a church has in a community is through its members in the workplaces and neighborhoods where God places them. Acts 8:4 says, "Therefore those who were scattered went everywhere preaching the word." That's how the gospel multiplies. People are so amazed and grateful by what God has done in their lives that they can't help but talk about it on the job or over the backyard fence. In the Bible, whenever Jesus did something wonderful for someone, that person always ran to tell others. Some even disobeyed His command to keep quiet. It's a hallmark of being saved that we can't wait to tell others what God has done, and continues to do, for us.

Winning souls not only pleases God, but it is also one of the smartest things you can do. Proverbs 11:30 says, "He who wins souls is wise." Daniel 12:3 says, "Those who are wise shall shine…forever and ever." This is one of the most exciting truths in the Bible: God allows us to share in His most important work. "For the Son of Man has come to seek and to save that which was lost" (Luke 19:10). He could have done the work of spreading the gospel all on His own, but He chose to make us "workers together with Him" (2 Cor. 6:1).

I encourage you to set your sights on multiplying other people's dreams by introducing them to Jesus. Give of your time, energy, money, and love, but most importantly, give away the gospel whenever you have the opportunity. You will be following God's pattern of fruitfulness, and I guarantee that your dreams will be realized along the way.

Study Guide Questions

1. In what ways do you serve others? How does that service help other people's dreams? How does it advance your own dreams? Explain.

    _____

    _____

    _____

    _____

2. Do you feel you are generous enough with your money? Rate yourself on the scale below, 1 being not generous, 10 being very generous.

    1 2 3 4 5 6 7 8 9 10

    How do you intend to become more generous? Write three specific things you will do in this coming week.

    _____

    _____

    _____

    _____

3. How do you express love to those around you? With hugs? Gifts? Words? Cards? Money? Are you "spending" enough of the endless love inside of you? Make a plan to give away more of your love.

    _____

    _____

    _____

    _____

4. Have you ever led someone to Jesus? When? When was the last time you talked with an unbeliever about Jesus? What was the conversation like? What was the result?

    _____

    _____

    _____

    _____

5. How can you become a greater soulwinner than you are now? Write a plan of action to share the gospel with people in your life.

    _____

    _____

    _____

    _____

Reflections

DAY 1

Read and review the chapter material.

DAY 2

> [Paul] went into the synagogue and spoke boldly…
> reasoning and persuading concerning the things of the
> kingdom of God….And this continued for two years,
> so that all who dwelt in Asia heard the word of the Lord
> Jesus, both Jews and Greeks.
>
> —ACTS 19:8, 10

One time a young man came to our Easter program. He wasn't saved; in fact, he was a habitual drug user. His former pastor had told him, "You're never going to change." His doctor told his parents, "You may as well get used to it. Your son will be on drugs the rest of his life."

That young man came to see the laser light show we put on that Easter because he thought it would be spectacular if he watched it while high on drugs. God touched his heart that night, and he made a sincere decision to follow Christ. But he still couldn't kick the drug habit. He came up to me after service one day and said, "Pastor, I try to leave it behind, but I always go back."

My heart was moved by his plight, and I decided to devote a portion of my time to helping him. I told him, "You're going to make it. Next week I want you to find me after service and tell me you went one week without drugs." He agreed, and the next week he did just that.

We went another week, and another, then one month, two months, three months. I saw him every week and spent those few moments with him after service, and soon he was drug-free. Today he is one of the leaders in my church in Los Angeles.

I am convinced that the investment of time I made in his life helped him overcome that habit. What would have happened if I had referred him to a counseling center instead? What if I had brushed him off and wished him well, but not given him my time and attention? I could have easily excused myself by saying, "I have so much to do; I don't have time for every single person who needs it." But I have learned that time is one of the best investments you can make.

Time is a limited commodity. When you give it to someone, you are communicating to them their value and preciousness to God. Jesus gave the disciples His time. To this day I try to emulate that example by paying special attention to every person I meet. I personally answer every letter sent to me. I spend time with whomever I am with; I don't let my mind go elsewhere. I give my attention to people, because people are worth it.

To whom will you give your time today?

1.   Who went out of their way to spend time with you, and how did that make you feel special?

   _____

   _____

   _____

   _____

2. How generous are you with your time? Explain.

_____

_____

_____

_____

3. Who needs more of your time? Your kids? Your family? Friends? Husband or wife? Make a list of people, and write ideas about how to spend more time with them.

_____

_____

_____

_____

Meditate on the idea that our time is short and incredibly valuable, and then pray for wisdom in being a steward of time.

DAY 3

It is more blessed to give than to receive.

—ACTS 20:35

There is a man in my church who loves Christmastime. One year he decided to give away 100 bicycles to children who couldn't afford them. He enjoyed that so much that the next year he gave more, and then more, until he was giving away 350 bicycles to kids during the Christmas season in partnership with our church.

Even that wasn't enough. He called up a friend of his who wasn't even a Christian and explained the opportunity he had to partner with our church in Los Angeles to give away 450 bicycles. Together, they did just that, donating $10,000 and making Christmas bright for all those families.

He discovered the blessing of giving his money away. People often quote Jesus that it's more blessed to give than to receive, but how many of us live it? It took me years to realize that this is not just a nice sentiment but a hard economic reality. If I give, I am more blessed than if I receive. I am happier, wealthier, more at peace, and less selfish.

That makes me want to give away everything I can to other people!

I know one man who is a major distributor of food in the U.S. and abroad. He is so wealthy that he owns ships. But he lives in the back of one of his several warehouses. He told me, "One day God gave me a dream and told me, 'Don't keep anything even for a day. Give it as fast as it comes in. You are not its keeper but its distributor.'"

That's what I want to be—a distributor, not a hoarder. A channel, not a reservoir. I want to fully learn the blessing of giving.

1.   Are you more of a distributor or a hoarder? Explain.

_____

_____

_____

_____

2.   What would be the practical result if you became wildly generous? Do you think you would go broke? Or do you think you would become wealthier? Explain your thoughts.

_____

_____

_____

_____

3.   What can you do today to set a pattern of greater generosity in your life?

_____

_____

_____

_____

Pray that you would fully understand and live in the blessing of giving.

DAY 4

No one will be able to stand up against you all the days of your life. As I was with Moses, so I will be with you.

—JOSHUA 1:5, NIV

One of the great secrets of reaching your dream is to serve someone else's dream—your boss, your pastor, your husband or wife, your mother or father. It's an iron law of leadership that you don't attain authority until you have served someone else's dream.

I can point to literally dozens of ministries that were started at my church by people who first served my dream. After a while, God gave each a unique dream and the opportunity to carry it out. Today at least half a dozen such ministries have gained national prominence and are touching thousands, even hundreds of thousands, of lives. Each began at my church.

These people "graduated" successfully from serving someone else's dream to reaching their own dream. They are like two great figures in the Old Testament, Joshua and Elisha. Joshua was one of Israel's strongest, most godly leaders. God gave him the privilege of leading the Israelites into the Promised Land. But for years, Joshua served Moses' dream. Those were years of training, observing, and growing in wisdom. At the right time God raised up Joshua and made him great.

Elisha was the long-time protégé of Elijah, a great prophet in the Old Testament. Elisha traveled with him, served him, and carried out his will. When Elijah went to be with the Lord, Elisha was given the mantle to carry on Elijah's work, so that the other prophets said:

> "The spirit of Elijah is resting on Elisha." And they went to meet him and bowed to the ground before him.
>
> —2 KINGS 2:15, NIV

The Bible records twice as many miracles done by Elisha as done by Elijah.

Before you reach your dream, you almost certainly will go through a season of serving someone else's dream. Here's how to do it well: Work for that person's dream as if it were your own. Give it your best thoughts and energy. Be selfless in your pursuit of excellence on their behalf. When you learn the lessons of that season, God will raise you up, and you will find yourself much closer to fulfilling your dream.

1. How would you describe your behavior under other people's authority? Are you a good servant? Are you resistant?

   _____

   _____

   _____

   _____

2. What season are you in now? Are you in season of learning or leading?

   _____

   _____

   _____

   _____

Pray that you would learn to serve other people's dreams so that your own dream would come to pass.

DAY 5

My God shall supply all your need according to His riches in glory.

—PHILIPPIANS 4:19

Are you at a place of perfect peace in regard to money? Your time? Your energy level? Are you completely free of worry about things like paying the bills, buying food, or putting gas in the car? If not, I can almost guarantee that you are not giving away your time, money, and energy. There is a direct correlation between your level of anxiety and the level of your generosity. Being anxious is a way of disbelieving God, and that reflects immediately in people's generosity—or lack of it. When you fear losing what you have, you grab it tighter.

But when you are at peace, your grip loosens and you give freely of your time, finances, and energy. Not only does giving your resources away please God, but it also shapes and transforms your mind so that you stop thinking in terms of what you don't have and start thinking in terms of the kingdom, which has inexhaustible supply.

Giving may be the only activity that releases us from concern about finances, time, and energy. It reminds us that God is behind it all. When you overwork because of greed or anxiety, your mind focuses too much on money, and you develop a mentality of scarcity. When you are stingy with your time, all you can think about is how little time you have. When you tell yourself how tired you are, you just become more tired.

But when you give, you reject the idea of scarcity. Your mind dwells on God and upon His goodness to you and to every living thing. That's why Jesus said:

Consider the lilies of the field, how they grow: they neither toil nor spin; and yet I say to you that even Solomon in all his glory was not arrayed like one of these.

—MATTHEW 6:28–29

When we think about the flowers or the birds, we realize God keeps them alive and beautiful by His abundance. Would He treat us any less?

If you are worried about not having enough, consider the evidence in nature itself. Thinking about the flowers outside your window will teach you more about God's provision than worrying about how to pay the bills. Lean on God's abundance, not on your own ability.

1. Where do you look for your supply? Be honest with yourself. Is it your job? Your pension? Your spouse's job? Does it strike mortal fear in you to think of that source being cut off? Explain.

_____

_____

_____

_____

2. Have you ever surrendered your finances to God's control? If not, write a prayer granting Him full control and access to your money.

_____

_____

_____

_____

DAY 6

> Let no debt remain outstanding, except the continuing debt to love one another, for he who loves his fellowman has fulfilled the law.
>
> —ROMANS 13:8, NIV

My dad showed love in many ways, and one was by planning adventures for me. One summer when I was nine years old he put me on a train, the Rock Island Zephyr, and told the conductor, "Don't let him off until he gets to Bowie, Texas."

My grandparents were supposed to meet me at the other end, but they were late, so the stationmaster asked me, "Who sent you here?"

"My dad," I said.

"Why?" he asked.

I answered, "Because he loves me, and he planned this great adventure for me."

My grandparents arrived, and I spent two months with them on their ranch, hauling water in from the city and dodging rattlesnakes, scorpions, and coyotes. I had a real adventure.

How do you show love? Some people give gifts; some give time; some give hugs. It doesn't matter how you show love as long as the person you are showing it to recognizes that it is love and that it is sincere and from your heart.

When my children were small, I had to learn their "love languages." Kristie loved receiving gifts from me. Luke liked being hugged, patted on the back, and told he was loved. Matthew enjoyed spending time just hanging out and talking. I consciously tried to love each one in the way he or she most appreciated.

I also learned that love is limitless. You can never lose love by giving it away. I decided to start giving love away all the time—I call it enlarging your circle of love so that nobody is on the outside. An amazing thing happened: My capacity to love grew. My experience of love grew. The feeling of love ballooned inside of me. The more I loved others, the more I was able to love them, and as a side benefit, I received more love in return.

Love is "dream fuel." Nothing makes people come alive quite like it. Make sure you are giving more than your share away.

1.   Who are the people in your life who need to hear you love them? What are their "love languages"?

_____

_____

_____

_____

2. Are you giving away as much love as you can, or is your pool of love stagnant? What would your life be like if you began loving people as if your love were without limits?

    _____

    _____

    _____

    _____

3. How do you like to be loved? Who loves you best? How?

    _____

    _____

    _____

    _____

Pray that God would teach you to love and that you would use all the love you have so you might receive more.

DAY 7

> [Jesus said,] "Therefore go and make disciples of all nations, baptizing them in the name of the Father and of the Son and of the Holy Spirit, and teaching them to obey everything I have commanded you."
>
> —MATTHEW 28:19–20, NIV

When I was a young evangelist, I rode with a pastor to the church where I was preaching at a meeting that night. The place was filled with cars, but as we pulled into the parking lot, the pastor's face turned fire engine red, and he began blustering.

"What's wrong?" I said.

He replied, "Somebody took my parking place!"

He was furious. Some poor sinner had mistakenly parked in his reserved spot.

Have you found yourself easily angered by "sinners"? Are you annoyed by their actions? Their waywardness? The mistakes they make? Some of us Christians look down on people who don't know Christ when we should be building bridges to them, finding common ground to stand on so we can share the gospel with love and sincerity. To multiply your dream, you must bring people to Jesus, who is the source of every dream.

How can you bring people to Christ? Does the idea of a one-on-one conversation about spiritual things scare you? Here's one way to approach it: talk about your relationship with God in the context of your goals and dreams. Few things are more attractive than a person, a church, or a small group with a God-given vision. It energizes outsiders and draws them in. When you are excited about your dream, people at work and in your family will be interested. They will ask you why you have such focus, such joy, and such hope for the future. Your dream will naturally open up avenues of conversation about Jesus.

I have said that if I could choose one word to describe me, it might very well be *soulwinner*. This should be our ambition, to draw people to Christ by going after our dreams with the peace, energy, and joy only He can give.

1. What is your default attitude toward non-Christians? Friendly? Condescending? Pitying? Loving? Explain.

    _____

    _____

    _____

    _____

2. When was the last time you talked with a non-Christian about Jesus? What was the conversation like? Explain.

    _____

    _____

    _____

    _____

3. What steps do you need to take to become a better soul-winner?

    _____

    _____

    _____

    _____

Pray that God would give you the opportunities and boldness to win souls.

CHAPTER FIVE

Dream With the Holy Spirit

*I*t might surprise you that the most important person involved in your dream is not you—it's the Holy Spirit. He is, in all likelihood, more interested in you fulfilling your dream than you are. Yet few of us know the Holy Spirit or live with a daily awareness of Him. Even fewer partner with Him to fulfill their dreams, and yet that is what we must do to attain them. For many years I ignored and grieved the Holy Spirit even though I grew up and pastored in a denomination that emphasizes the work and baptism of the Holy Spirit. What I didn't realize is that:

1. The Holy Spirit is a person.

2. We should talk with Him more than we talk with anyone else on earth.

3. He has been given the responsibility and power to help our dreams come to pass.

Let me share briefly my experience with the Holy Spirit and what I learned about partnering with Him to reach my own dreams.

My first experience with the Holy Spirit was when I was saved at age four, praying in the family car with my mother. Even though I was young, it felt as if a thousand pounds were lifted off my shoulders at that moment, and because I had accepted Christ, the Holy Spirit came to dwell within me. Later on, when I was thirteen, I was baptized in the Holy Spirit. (See Acts 2.) I was endued with power I had not known, and I became bold for God in a new way, where previously I had been ashamed to be known as a preacher's kid. Three years later, at age sixteen, I began to evangelize, and God gave me great success in the U.S. and around the world. In 1970 I started pastoring my first church, in Davenport, Iowa.

But it wasn't until I was over forty years old, pastoring my current church in Phoenix, that I came to know the Holy Spirit as a person instead of an experience or some mysterious heavenly force. Up until then I knew Him theologically, legalistically, and experientially, but not personally. In fact, I had even questioned the Holy Spirit and His work because of what I had seen in the church. The Holy Spirit was supposed to make people holy, godly, and effective witnesses, but some of the people I observed who were filled with the Holy Spirit were also the meanest, most controlling, and least fruitful Christians I knew. They never won people to the Lord. They did not have the spiritual depth or character I thought they should have.

But after I searched the Scriptures, I concluded that being filled with the Holy Spirit was real. There was no getting around it. So I sought God and asked Him to open my eyes so I could understand what this should mean for me and the church I was leading. I wanted to be a Spirit-filled church, whatever that meant in practice.

Then I had a life-changing encounter with the Holy Spirit in a telephone booth one day. I used to have a radio show called *The Pastor's Phone Call,* in which I would call the local radio station at noon on a particular day from wherever I was. Sometimes I would call from an airport, a gas station, a hospital, or the house of a church member, and I would give a short, uplifting sermon. On this day I called the radio station from a telephone booth and preached about the Holy Spirit. I told that radio audience, "The Holy Spirit dwells within us. He's alive, He's here, and He's real." Suddenly, it dawned on me for the very first time that the Holy Spirit was indeed real and was a person. The awe-inspiring presence of God came upon me, and I trembled as I continued. I had a strong sense that the Holy Spirit was present and was listening to me. I had never had such an awareness before. I instinctively straightened my tie and buttoned my coat, as if in the presence of a great dignitary. I finished my radio message, went to my car, and got on my knees, thoroughly shaken. I said, "Holy Spirit, I realize You are here. You are ever with me. You are a person, and You are real. I want You to forgive me. You have been right beside me all these years, and I haven't acknowledged You. I've talked to God the Father and to Jesus, but I've never spoken a word to You. I'm not going to make that mistake again. I love You; I depend on You. Let's go and work together."

Beginning that day, I changed how I approached life, in big things and little things. I used to read the newspaper an hour a day, first thing in the morning. But now I talked with the Holy Spirit first, then read my newspaper, and talked to Him some more while I read. I began to talk with Him all the time, asking Him about which tie to wear, which route to take to church. I found myself taking different routes. One day I found a man with a flat tire and invited him to church, and he was later saved.

I consulted with the Holy Spirit about big decisions I made regarding my church and its many ministries. I discovered how to live in constant partnership with the Holy Spirit, talking to Him throughout the day, saying things like, "Holy Spirit, I recognize You and ask You to guide my steps. Bring me in contact with people I need to speak with and be with me today. I ask You to take control of my life." The Holy Spirit became my senior pastor and senior partner in everything I did. As a result, new thoughts and creative ideas have poured into my life. I have been able to build ministries and do things I couldn't have done on my own.

Not only that, but He settled a struggle I had carried with me throughout my life—a struggle to find deep, abiding peace. Early in my ministry as a pastor, I would easily get upset and worry about everything in the church. I was quick to anger and never had a pervasive sense of peace. But with the Holy Spirit in my life, I suddenly had peace. I was comforted, not discomforted. That peace revolutionized my life. I now have a different approach to my life and my church that comes from knowing deep down that I am not alone in my task. My Helper has come! He is the Holy Spirit, my constant delight.

WHO IS HE TO YOU?

I wonder if you are able to say the same thing. Is the Holy Spirit a real person to you? Is He your constant companion, your partner, your delight? Coming to know the Holy Spirit as a person was one of the single most transforming experiences of my life, next to salvation and discovering how to pray. We Christians have been given a wonderful gift of relationship with this third member of the Trinity, and yet so few of us know what it is to have a relationship with Him. Even though He dwells within us, we have no fellowship with Him. We never address Him directly. We don't partner with Him in our dreams, seek His advice, or run our ideas by Him. For the average believer, the Holy Spirit is more an idea than a person.

For people who grew up in Pentecostal churches, the Holy Spirit is often a one-time experience, a strange but welcome enduement of power that took place at an altar or a youth camp. When I was baptized in the Holy Spirit, I knew Him as a force unlike any I had known. I knew I had received the greatest power in the universe, but I didn't know the person behind the power. I didn't know Him as a personal Comforter. And neither do many Christians to this day.

I believe some of us wish we didn't have to bother with the Holy Spirit. We think it would be easier if we didn't have to accommodate Him in our lives. Some people probably even get annoyed by the idea of the Holy Spirit as a person we must relate to. It almost seems better if we pray to the Father and not bother with getting to know this other member of the Trinity.

But Jesus said it was better that the Holy Spirit come. I've often wondered, *How could anything be better than Jesus Himself?* I imagine the disciples thought the same thing when

Jesus told them He was returning to the Father. This news must have shocked and saddened those twelve men who had given up everything to follow Him. Jesus said He was leaving and someone else would take His place. I don't know about you, but I would not have wanted "another Comforter" Jesus spoke of. I would have wanted the first Comforter, Jesus. That would have been good enough for me. How could anyone else fill His shoes? But Jesus knew there was a better way. The Holy Spirit would dispense on a global scale the blessings Jesus won to mankind on the cross. Jesus conquered sin, sickness, and the devil, but in His earthly ministry, He confined himself to about a seventy-mile radius and His physical body to be in one place at a time. Going from one place to another took much time. But the Holy Spirit could be everywhere at the same time. He is a person, but He is also a spirit. He could move in people's hearts with much greater freedom of time and space than a man could.

The Holy Spirit came to carry out the work Jesus began and demonstrated while in His earthly body. The presence of the Holy Spirit is the very presence of Jesus Christ. And because He took the place of Jesus and was not inferior in any way, we know this about Him:

1. The Holy Spirit is a person, not a thing.

2. The Comforter possesses Jesus' qualities.

3. The Holy Spirit does the same things Jesus did.

The Holy Spirit is a person, not a thing.

A thing could never take the place of a person. Jesus was a person, so the Comforter He sent would have to be a person as well. For this reason, we can never treat the Holy Spirit like a thing. He is not an "it." He is a relational being. He has knowledge, wisdom, emotion, and volition. He has a distinct personality to which we can relate.

The Comforter possesses Jesus' qualities.

If He were lesser than Jesus, He would have never filled Jesus' place, and the church would have disintegrated long ago. His abilities would have to be as great as Jesus' abilities, or Jesus would not have said it was better that the Holy Spirit come.

The Holy Spirit does the same things Jesus did.

Jesus loved us, so the Holy Spirit loves us, too. Jesus healed people, taught people, gave them wisdom, cast out devils, comforted His followers, raised the dead, and performed miracles— and so does the Holy Spirit! His agenda is exactly the same as Jesus' agenda.

It's encouraging to know that the Holy Spirit is the spirit of Christ. He carries out Christ's work in the world and in our hearts.

WHAT THE HOLY SPIRIT DOES

What else does the Holy Spirit do, according to the Bible?

1. He draws people to Jesus.

The Bible says no one comes to God, but the Holy Spirit draws him. That is His primary mission on earth. Whenever you speak to the lost about Jesus, the Holy Spirit is there saying, "That's right. Listen to this." The Spirit bears witness to the truth. (That should take all the fear out of your heart about soul-winning!)

2. He brings things to our remembrance.

Jesus said the Holy Spirit would lead us into all truth (John 16:13). The Bible also says we have the mind of Christ (1 Cor. 2:16). The Holy Spirit is the gatekeeper of all knowledge and wisdom of God, as the Bible says:

> For the Spirit searches all things, yes, the deep things of God.
>
> —1 CORINTHIANS 2:10

You may have a college education and a doctorate degree, but if you are not filled with the Holy Spirit, your education is limited. He will lead you into all truth.

    3. He helps us to pray.

The Bible says that when we pray in the Spirit, we pray in groanings we know not of (Rom. 8:26). We'll talk about this more later in this chapter, and I'll tell you how your prayer life can be revolutionized with His help.

    4. He reveals things to us we wouldn't normally know.

In the Old Testament, the most feared men were the prophets because the Holy Spirit would reveal things to them. The enemies of God thought the people of God had spies because the Holy Spirit would reveal to the Israelites their strategies and plans of attack. The prophet Daniel wrote, "There is a God in heaven who reveals secrets" (Dan. 2:28).

    5. He baptizes us and gives us spiritual gifts.

6. He anoints us for the task and dreams we have
   been called to.

This means that when we accept a new responsibility or embark on a new adventure, He gives us spiritual understanding to carry it out. The Bible says:

> He who has an ear, let him hear what the Spirit says
> to the churches.
>
> —REVELATION 2:7

The Holy Spirit will give you the ability to see things through God's eyes, and comprehend things the natural man doesn't comprehend. He will give you wisdom, discernment, power, and insight to make decisions and accomplish your highest, most challenging goals.

THE HOLY SPIRIT, YOUR PRAYER PARTNER

When you get to know the Holy Spirit, He also becomes your prayer partner. I have discovered in six decades of learning to pray that I don't always know what I need. I don't always know what to pray for. Sometimes I know what I think I need, but I might ask for something that, if I got it, would destroy my life or ministry. I need somebody who can help me, who knows what I need before I even bring my requests to the Father.

Most of my prayer time is spent thanking and praising God, and just being with Him like a best friend, as I described earlier. But there come times for each of us when we need to go boldly before the throne of grace and say, "God, I have a need. Today I have to do some asking, seeking, and knocking."

The good news is that when we approach the Father, we are not alone. The Holy Spirit is with us. Going to the Father can be an intimidating experience for some people. When I was a boy and had a need, I would sometimes be afraid to ask my dad for it, so I would go to my mother first and tell her the need. We would talk about it, and I would ask her to go with me to my dad. She would tell him, "Tommy's been a good boy. He's gotten good grades in school. He minds us so much and practices his music." My mom would intercede for me with my dad, just as the Holy Spirit intercedes for us in prayer.

Romans 8:27 tells us:

> Now He who searches the hearts knows what the mind of the Spirit is, because He makes intercession for the saints according to the will of God.

I have learned to make the Holy Spirit my prayer partner. I talk to Him before I petition the Father, and I say, "Holy Spirit, in a moment I'm going to the Father with my petitions, but since You're my prayer partner, I'm going to run them by You first. I don't know what I need, but You do." Then I list my prayers and needs, and He responds about what I need or don't need. He filters out my wrong or misguided requests. Then I get a piece of paper and make a list of what I feel He is telling me to pray for. Then I go to God the Father with my petitions.

Some people have asked me, "Tommy, do you ever stand on Matthew 21:22, which says you can receive anything you want in prayer?" Yes, I believe in that promise. You can choose to say to God, "I will have this, Lord," and demand it. But I am very aware of my own lack of knowledge about what I really need, which is why I more often pray, "Not my will, but Thine, Lord.

Surprise me. I've told You what I want, but if You have some-thing better, give it to me." As a result, God has given me things I didn't even know I desired—things that made me so happy but which I had never considered.

Not only does the Holy Spirit help us edit our prayer requests, but He also supplies the supernatural ability to communicate with God beyond the language we understand. My experience with prayer is that I can pray for a short while in English, and then I run out of things to say. That's when the Holy Spirit takes over and I express myself to God "with groans that words can-not express" (Rom. 8:26, NIV). In those moments the Holy Spirit tells the Father what I need, and God understands the mysteries I speak through the Spirit. The result is a wonderful sense of peace and calm, as Paul tells us in this same passage:

> And we know that all things work together for good to
> those who love God.
>
> —ROMANS 8:28

This comment immediately follows the teaching about the Holy Spirit's intercession, and the two are directly related. The word *and* means this thought is connected to the previous thought, meaning you cannot get to "in all things God works for the good of those who love him, who have been called according to his purpose" until you go through "the Spirit himself inter-cedes for us with groans that words cannot express" (NIV).

Your prayer partner, the Holy Spirit, gives you a hotline to the heart of God.

GETTING TO KNOW THE HOLY SPIRIT

I hope your heart has opened up to this relationship you can have with the Holy Spirit. He jealously desires you, as the Bible says in James 4:5: "The Spirit who dwells in us yearns jealously." Why does He desire you so much? Because you belong to Him!

> Or do you not know that your body is the temple of the Holy Spirit who is in you, whom you have from God, and you are not your own?
> —1 CORINTHIANS 6:19

Your body belongs to Him. Your mind belongs to Him. Your dreams belong to Him, and only He can help you bring them to fulfillment. He will steer you around potential hazards, give you creative ideas, bring you favor with other people, and bless you financially by giving you insightful ideas you can use to your advantage.

He will become more than your prayer partner; He will be your dream partner. This partnership will be one of the greatest experiences of your life. Of course, no relationship can grow with only one encounter. Your relationship with Him should be daily, even hourly. You should commune with the Holy Spirit. Recognize Him. Speak with Him. Love Him. Talk to Him. He will guide and build your dreams much better than you can.

Study Guide Questions

1. What kind of church were you raised in, if any, and how did this shape your view of the Holy Spirit? How do you view the Holy Spirit and His role in your life today?

   _____

   _____

   _____

   _____

2. What is your relationship with the Holy Spirit?

   _____

   _____

   _____

   _____

3. How has your relationship with the Holy Spirit changed your life over the long term? What would you consider the closest encounter you have ever had to experiencing an enduement of His power?

   _____

   _____

   _____

   _____

4. Talk about the Holy Spirit's role in prayer and how you plan to include Him as a prayer partner. How do you think this would change the way you talk to God?

_____

_____

_____

_____

5. How will you give yourself more fully to the Holy Spirit this week? Start each day by talking with Him. Be prepared next week to share with the group the changes you experienced as a result of your relationship with the Holy Spirit.

_____

_____

_____

_____

Reflections

DAY 1

Read and review the chapter material.

DAY 2

> It is to your advantage that I [Jesus] go away; for if I
> do not go away, the Helper will not come to you; but
> if I depart, I will send Him to you.
>
> —JOHN 16:7, NKJV

Before I got married, I had a longstanding habit when I traveled. I would get up, buy a newspaper, and read it over a cup of coffee. On my honeymoon, I got up the first morning and went down to the restaurant with my new bride, Marja. We sat down, and I unfolded the newspaper and read it while she sat there. This went on for several mornings until one morning she became quiet and sad.

I said, "What's wrong with you? You're on your honeymoon. I'm taking you around the world. Why are you acting this way?"

She said to me, "I don't want to be treated like an it or a thing. Why don't you lay down that newspaper and treat me like a person?"

I learned then that people don't like to be treated like things. I had to adjust to her presence in my life. I couldn't behave the way I did when I was single, expecting her to fit into my pre-established routine. Like all people, she wanted someone to speak to her, appreciate her, gaze upon her, and laugh and cry with her. She wanted *relationship*.

The Holy Spirit is a person, too. He is knowledgeable, wise, sensitive, and powerful, but He is also delicate, has deep emotions, a personality, and a character. He wishes to relate to you as a person.

For many years, I neglected relationship with the Holy Spirit and went about my routines of ministry. I grieved Him in the same way I would have grieved my new wife had I ignored her and continued to read my newspaper.

Too many followers of Christ know the Holy Spirit as an experience or something to be received, but they don't know Him as a person. They want to tack Him on to their lives without changing their routines. But to achieve your dream, you will need relationship with the Holy Spirit. Don't try to experience Him or use Him; rather, love Him, recognize Him daily and hourly, adore Him, praise Him, and seek Him. Build the relationship that will become your very source and stability as you follow your dreams.

1. How would you characterize your present relationship with the Holy Spirit? In what way could you improve the manner in which you relate to the Holy Spirit?

    _____

    _____

    _____

    _____

2.   What kind of relationship do you envision having with the Holy Spirit? Explain in detail.

_____

_____

_____

_____

Talk to the Holy Spirit in prayer, confessing that you have not paid attention to Him and asking for wisdom to build a life-changing relationship with Him.

DAY 3

> Then the churches throughout all Judea, Galilee, and Samaria had peace and were edified. And walking in the fear of the Lord and in the comfort of the Holy Spirit, they were multiplied.
>
> —ACTS 9:31

Driving home from work one day after a downpour, a friend of mine saw a little old lady alongside the road who had fallen into a mud puddle. Torn grocery bags were strewn around her, and she was trying to get up. He stopped the car, ran back, and discovered she was skinned and bruised.

At first, she was suspicious of this man running to help her, but he brushed her off and said, "Let me take you home."

She looked at him warily and said, "I don't know."

He assured her he was a Christian and had no intent to harm

her, so she got into his car. He drove her to her apartment, carried the groceries in for her, and said good-bye. She tried to give him money for his trouble, but he refused. A few weeks later, she sent him a wonderful letter of thanks.

That friend of mine gave comfort when comfort was needed. So does the Holy Spirit give us comfort when we need it. Everyone feels helpless and scattered sometimes, as if we have fallen into the mud with our dreams scattered about us. Those times are confusing, and even humiliating, but that's when the Holy Spirit comes alongside us, picks us up, and leads us on.

That comfort of the Holy Spirit does more than we might expect; it multiplies the work of God. The Bible says, "In the comfort of the Holy Spirit, they [the churches] were multiplied." Comfort is a key ingredient for growing your dream. Comfort is the opposite of stressed-out and harassed. Comfort also implies there will be adverse events and circumstances for which we will need the Holy Spirit's comfort.

But when we receive that comfort, our work and dreams will multiply.

1. When was the last time you felt the comfort of the Holy Spirit?

    _____

    _____

    _____

    _____

This week, think of someone in your small group or church who is in need of comfort. Pray and ask the Holy Spirit to use you as an instrument of comfort in that person's life. Take the time to listen to His voice and direction.

DAY 4

It seemed good to the Holy Ghost, and to us.

—ACTS 15:28, KJV

I was fielding questions at a men's breakfast one Saturday morning when a man asked me a question that set me back on my heels. He said, "Why don't you preach more on the Holy Spirit?"

I began to think about it. I knew I mentioned the Holy Spirit in every sermon, but the man was right—I rarely spoke about Him at length. That has changed dramatically, and in the last few years I have wanted to speak only about the Holy Spirit. The reason is the transformation I experienced in relating to the Holy Spirit, where He has become a person and a personal comforter to me.

But He became something more: He has become my counselor. I make no decision without consulting Him. He is the CEO of my life and my church. I am second to Him in every decision I make. I constantly ask if my ideas and plans "seem good to the Holy Spirit," and I submit to His leadership.

This is how your relationship with the Holy Spirit was designed to be. He should be your senior partner. He wants to be active in your life and dreams today just as He was in the lives of the first Christians. Peter and the other apostles declared this when they said:

We are His [Jesus'] witnesses to these things, and so also is the Holy Spirit whom God has given to those who obey Him.

—ACTS 5:32

They described the Holy Spirit as working right alongside them. When they chose workers within the church, they looked for people "full of the Holy Spirit" (Acts 6:3). And before they embarked on great ministry ventures, they waited on the Holy Spirit, who let them know what He wanted. One time, "as they ministered to the Lord, and fasted, the Holy Ghost said, Separate me Barnabas and Saul for the work whereunto I have called them" (Acts 13:2, KJV).

1. In what way is the Holy Spirit your CEO and counselor? How and when do you seek His wisdom? Explain.

_____

_____

_____

_____

2. Envision your life with the Holy Spirit as your senior partner and counselor. How would your decision-making process change?

_____

_____

_____

_____

Pray that the Holy Spirit would have full reign in your life.

DAY 5

> In the same way, the Spirit helps us in our weakness. We do not know what we ought to pray for, but the Spirit himself intercedes for us with groans that words cannot express.
>
> —ROMANS 8:26, NIV

There came a time in my prayer life when I realized I didn't know what to pray for. I didn't know what I needed. I didn't even know what I wanted. The realization surprised me, even though I should have figured it out much sooner. After all, Paul wrote plainly, "We do not know what we ought to pray for." But for a long time I *thought* I knew what I wanted and needed from God. I *thought* I knew how to approach Him in prayer. In fact, I was neglecting the Holy Spirit's partnership in prayer, and I believe I limited my effectiveness in prayer.

From that time on I have respected the Holy Spirit's role in my prayer life. I "consult" with Him before bringing my requests before the Father. I allow Him to lead me "into all truth" concerning my wants and needs. He has shown me wants, needs, and dreams I didn't know I had. I discover them in my interaction with the Holy Spirit during prayer, and then I lay those dreams and petitions before the Father, and the Holy Spirit even then intercedes for me in ways that words cannot express.

Do you know what you need? Do you know what you want? Do you know how to pray? If you answered *no* to any or all those questions, you are in a perfect position! The Holy Spirit wants to begin a partnership with you, to help you in your weakness, and to interact with you in prayer so you better understand your wants, needs, and dreams. Welcome Him as your prayer partner, your intercessor. It will transform your prayer life.

1. When was the last time you consulted with the Holy Spirit about your wants and needs, if ever? What was the result? How different was your perceived idea of what you thought you needed from what you truly needed?

_____

_____

_____

_____

2. What is the Holy Spirit's part in your present prayer life? Is He central to your prayers, or is He on the sidelines?

_____

_____

_____

_____

Day 6

Ask the Lord of the harvest, therefore, to send out workers into his harvest field.

—Matthew 9:38, niv

When I was a pastor in Davenport, Iowa, my church took a strong stand against massage parlors and adult bookstores that had sprung up in town. Several young men stood in front of the stores handing out Christian literature and telling every person who left the store, "Jesus loves you."

One day a man came out of the adult bookstore, and our young man smiled and said, "Jesus loves you." The man was so angry that he hauled off and hit the boy in the mouth, knocking him down and busting his lip. The young man stood back up and said, "Mister, Jesus still loves you."

The angry man went home and tried to sleep, but his mind was filled with thoughts of his mother and of the old country preacher he had grown up hearing. He couldn't get the image of the young man saying "Jesus loves you" out of his head, so finally he knelt by his bed and gave his heart to Jesus. The next Wednesday he showed up at church, and during the testimony time he told his story.

That man's story is a perfect example of the Holy Spirit's primary work on this planet. He draws people to Jesus. The Holy Spirit wouldn't leave that man alone. That's because the Holy Spirit is the Lord of the harvest. He convicts people of sin and convinces them of their need for a Savior. Jesus said, "The Spirit of truth, who proceeds from the Father...will testify of Me" (John 15:26).

The Holy Spirit's job is to get people to understand the truth. Jesus called Him the "Spirit of truth," and said, "He will guide you into all truth" (John 16:13).

The first step in knowing the truth is accepting Jesus. The next step is to share that truth with others, because the Spirit of truth now lives in you. If you are not spreading the truth of God's Word and Jesus' love to people around you, the Holy Spirit is probably not fully operating in your life. The proof of His presence is that people are being drawn to God.

I pray that is true of you!

1. How did the Holy Spirit work in your life to bring you to Jesus?

    _____

    _____

    _____

    _____

2. How does the Holy Spirit speak to others through your words and actions? How can you better partner with Him to bring in a harvest of souls?

    _____

    _____

    _____

    _____

Pray for sensitivity to the Holy Spirit's leading so you can accomplish things together with Him.

DAY 7

> "Not by might nor by power, but by My Spirit," says the LORD of hosts.
>
> —ZECHARIAH 4:6

When I was a boy, God called me to preach, and that became my dream and my passion. I gave my first sermon to an adult congregation at age sixteen. I was skinny and short, and I had terrible acne. Although I was inferior by many outside measures, I prayed, "God, I've never preached. I'm not much to look at. You have to help me." That week I preached, and many people were saved. I asked God for new sermons every day, because I only had one to start with. He gave me more, and I seemed to have success everywhere I went. People came to the meetings, and many gave their lives to the Lord. Some of the campaigns went on for weeks.

But then I held a series of meetings that went on for a week, and nobody was saved. I finally got on my knees and said, "God, why have You forsaken me? I left my mother and father to come down to Texas to preach. Now You have left me." I opened my eyes and saw a scripture posted in the room I was in. I believe it was there by divine purpose. It was Zechariah 4:6: "'Not by might nor by power, but by My Spirit,' says the LORD of hosts."

I learned then, and I have relearned many times since, that you will never make it far in your dream without the help of the Holy Spirit. He is the administrator of all your potential. He counsels you, comforts you, and endues you with power and wisdom. Every morning He supplies fresh energy, ideas, and encouragement to get you moving forward somehow.

Without Him, your dream is dead in the water. Jesus said of Himself, "The Spirit of the LORD is upon Me" (Luke 4:18). The disciples too "were filled with joy and with the Holy Spirit" (Acts 13:52).

Jesus and the disciples were unable to carry out their dreams without the ongoing, active participation of the Holy Spirit. The same is true for us. Our dreams will go nowhere without Him. But with Him, we can do anything!

1. Who is in charge of your dream, you or the Holy Spirit? Explain the division of labor you have with Him now and how you think that should change, if at all.

    _____

    _____

    _____

    _____

2. What are the specific signs in your life that your partnership and relationship with the Holy Spirit are alive and active? What are the signs that you are losing touch with the Holy Spirit?

    _____

    _____

    _____

    _____

Ask the Holy Spirit to fill you with joy and power for the tasks you have today.

CHAPTER SIX

There's a Miracle Dream in
Your House

*J*ust as God gave us the Holy Spirit, He gives us all the resources
and abilities we need to fulfill our dreams. God never gives us
dreams without giving us the tools to make them possible. Not
only is there a dream in your house, but there is a miracle in your
house to fulfill it.

What does it mean to have "a miracle in your house"? Second
Kings 4:1–7 shows us in the circumstance of a widow whose creditor was about to take her two children away from her because she
had run out of money.

> A certain woman of the wives of the sons of the
> prophets cried out to Elisha, saying, "Your servant

my husband is dead, and you know that your servant feared the LORD. And the creditor is coming to take my two sons to be his slaves."

So Elisha said to her, "What shall I do for you? Tell me, what do you have in the house?" And she said, "Your maidservant has nothing in the house but a jar of oil."

Then he said, "Go, borrow vessels from everywhere, from all your neighbors—empty vessels; do not gather just a few. And when you have come in, you shall shut the door behind you and your sons; then pour it into all those vessels, and set aside the full ones."

So she went from him and shut the door behind her and her sons, who brought the vessels to her; and she poured it out. Now it came to pass, when the vessels were full, that she said to her son, "Bring me another vessel."

And he said to her, "There is not another vessel." So the oil ceased. Then she came and told the man of God. And he said, "Go, sell the oil and pay your debt; and you and your sons live on the rest."

This biblical example lays out the pattern for finding the miracle for your dream in your house.

First, we must find out what is in the house—what resources we have, what talents and experience, what contacts. Like that widow, we too often get caught up in what we don't have and lose sight of the provision God has already made available. The beginning of a miracle was literally in her kitchen, but she didn't see it because it was too small.

Some people think they have to rely on outside money, outside talent, or outside manpower to reach their dreams. They think the resources for accomplishing their dreams are in other people's hands, so they spend a lot of time trying to convince others to support them. But the opposite is really true. Each person reading this book has been given the resources, or access to the resources, to carry out his or her dream. Perhaps you think you have nothing—but that is simply never true. Every person has a mind, physical strength, experience, and knowledge. As a Christian, the Holy Spirit lives in your "house." Christ lives in your house, in all His omnipotence and omnipresence. God Himself indwells you; His resources are yours. Far from having nothing, you have everything. Second Peter 1:3 says:

> As His divine power has given to us all things that
> pertain to life and godliness, through the knowledge
> of Him who called us by glory and virtue.

You have everything you need. So what is in your house? Do an inventory assessment. List your talents, gifts, skills, and firsthand experience. List your bank account balance, investments, and property. List your friends, colleagues, contacts, and co-workers. Perhaps you are overlooking a small miracle that could easily grow into huge provision. Maybe you have an idea for a product, service, or business you consider interesting but probably insignificant. Did you know that every great corporation, every great work of God, every great invention began as a seemingly insignificant idea? Don't despise those small ideas. They may be the very thoughts God gave you! His intentions often come in the form of ideas that occur to you like sparks of creativity. I would venture to say that God has already shared ideas with you that could change your life and the world.

Miracles Surround You

Scour your house for potential. When I was a boy and wanted money to buy things, I started by asking my mom and dad for money. When that avenue was exhausted, I looked for other things in the house I could redeem. I found bottles I could sell at the recycler. I found stacks of newspapers I could sell by the pound to the salvage yard. I was amazed what I found in the house. There was always more than I expected.

This principle has held up throughout my life. When I went to pastor my first church in Davenport, I did not realize that the seed for a miracle was in that lackluster church of seventy-six people. The total annual income was almost nil. The people were relentlessly negative.

But God had a seed, an elderly woman who came to me one day and said, "I have only been saved a few months, but every week I go knocking on doors. I invite people to church and try to win them to Jesus Christ. Am I supposed to do that?"

I said, "You sure are."

Together, she, a small group, and I started canvassing neighborhoods every week. One day an old German brother found Jesus, and the next Sunday morning I seated him on the front row. I said, "Folks, we won somebody to the Lord last week. Stand up, Fred." He turned around and raised both hands with tears streaming down his cheeks. I announced, "We're going soul-winning next Thursday."

Four ladies showed up, and we went out witnessing. That day we won two very old ladies to the Lord. We brought them to church and introduced them in the service. Within weeks, many others were going out knocking on doors, and the whole front row filled up with new converts. Some people were making three trips every Sunday morning to bring people to church in their cars. Then someone donated a bus, and someone else bought one for us, and soon hundreds of people were arriving at church every Sunday on our buses, until we had forty-seven buses bringing more than three thousand people each week. We became America's fastest-growing church.

In that little, run-down "house" was the seed of a major harvest in Davenport!

I saw that happen again when I started a church in Los Angeles. For years I had dreamed of starting a church in that great city, but I had many doubts about whether I could handle it, how I would pastor my congregation in Phoenix and in L.A., and if I was too old to be starting something new. Finally, after two years of wrestling with the idea, I plunged ahead, but I needed someone to co-pastor with me. After searching and interviewing candidates for months, I had found no one who I felt was right to co-pastor with me in L.A. and run the operations when I was not there. Finally, a man in my church confronted me and said, "You've always said the miracle is in the house. Maybe the answer to your problem is your own son, Matthew." I didn't want to hear that at all! Matthew was twenty years old. Inner-city L.A. was dangerous. He was inexperienced. The challenge might eat him alive, but the more I prayed about it, the more I was convinced that the miracle was in my house. Matthew was the right person for the job.

Today, under Matthew's and my leadership, the Dream Center feeds and ministers to thirty thousand people a week and is making a dramatic impact in the inner city. The miracle was in my house. I'm glad God sent that man to tell me so, or I might have overlooked it.

A former professional football player in our church wanted to do something for God some years ago, so he looked at what was in his house. He had experience with athletes, and he knew their needs. So he started an athletes conference that grew to be the biggest conference of its kind, hosting major players each year. It began with an idea that was already in his house, and it grew to bless tens of thousands. Eventually the ministry had its own Olympic training site and sent fifteen athletes to the Olympic Games in Sydney, Australia in 2000. They won three gold medals, three silver medals, and two bronze medals.

Maybe the miracle in your house is your past career or your children. Maybe you have geniuses growing up right under your nose. Maybe your spouse is the miracle in your house. Maybe the job you already have or the business or ministry you already run is the key to your miracle.

ACTION

Once you have taken inventory, it's time to act. Elisha told the widow to get jars from all her neighbors, and she did it on faith. Most people want God to act on their behalf before they take a step of faith, but that's not how it works. You must act by faith first. We talked earlier about how God supplies power along the way. It takes faith, even just a little faith, to get started. In fact, everything you accomplish in this life will come by faith alone. You do not get things from God because you're a good Christian or because you love Him so much or because of your sweet disposition—you get things because of faith. Prayer alone does not get things from God. Neither does reading the Bible. Only faith gets things from God.

Faith means believing God more than we believe our five senses. Having faith does not mean being free of doubt. In fact, doubt is an essential part of faith. Think about it: if there were no doubt, there would be no faith. But faith means acting on the belief instead of on the doubt. The Bible says that every person has a measure of faith. God has already given it to us. There is no need to pray for greater faith. We only need to use the faith we have.

The Bible also speaks of "the power that works in us" (Eph. 3:20). The question you need to ask yourself is this: is that power working in you or is it merely residing in you? You may have tons of potential, but God does not act according to your potential. He acts according to your faith demonstrated by your actions. You see, power is usually the last thing to arrive. When God works in your dream, He gives three things:

1. A plan

2. A promise

3. Power

God gave Abraham the plan: "I want you to be father of a great nation." Then came a promise: "I'll multiply your offspring like the sand on the seashore." Last came the power to conceive at an old age.

God gave Moses a plan, "Free My people," a promise, "I'll be with you wherever you go," and the power to do miracles before Pharaoh.

Jesus gave the disciples a plan, "Go and make disciples of all nations," a promise, "I will be with you even to the end of the age," and the power (Acts 2). Do you see the sequence? The plan and promise always come before the power. The problem for many of us is that we want power first. One Christian prayed for years, "Give me more power, more power!" Finally God said, "With plans no bigger than yours, you don't need more power." Many people don't need the power of God to fulfill their plans. It's not enough to believe in miracles; you have to depend on them.

What you ask or think can put a limit upon God's power in your life. I would encourage you, don't limit God's ability to provide. Believe for the plan and promise of your dream, for the Lord said to the widow through the prophet, "Go borrow. Get as many vessels as you can." Even when things look small, plan big. Remember, the dream must be so big that if it becomes reality, everybody will know it had to be God.

Fill your house with expectancy. Conduct an inventory of what you have and whom you know. Then take action and start pouring! The best promise of the widow's story is that the miraculous supply of oil kept flowing until every vessel was filled. There is no shortage with God! He has put the seeds of a miracle in your house that will bring your dream into reality. Your "house" may be your church, your business, your school, your home, your workplace, your day-care center. All the creativity, finances, and resources for your dream are in that house in one form or another.

Dream big; then discover the miracle in your house!

Study Guide Questions

1. Have you ever felt powerless to fulfill the dream God placed in your heart? What caused you to feel this way? Have you sought the resources for a miracle outside your "house"? Explain.

    _____

    _____

    _____

    _____

2. Conduct a personal inventory. What gifts, talents, knowledge, resources, friendships, and connections do you have that would help you get started on your dream? Nothing is too small! List as many as you can.

    _____

    _____

    _____

    _____

3. How can you use these resources right now to progress toward your dream? What action can you take this week? Should you make a phone call to a colleague? Enroll in college courses? Write up a business plan? What will you do specifically?

    _____

    _____

    _____

    _____

4. Do you ever doubt your dream? Is your doubt bigger than your faith? Rate yourself below, 1 being "always doubtful" and 10 being "always full of faith."

    1 2 3 4 5 6 7 8 9 10

    How can you raise your faith level?

    _____

    _____

    _____

    _____

5. How would your dream change if you tried to dream bigger? Are you limiting God in your life by harboring small dreams? Explain.

_____

_____

_____

_____

Reflections

DAY 1

Read and review the chapter material.

DAY 2

> Tell me, what do you have in the house?
>
> —2 KINGS 4:2

Your dream always starts with what you have, not with what you do not have. Excuses don't make good foundations; neither do long lists of what you lack. Everybody has something, even if it's an idea, a strong body for labor, or a seemingly minor and mundane skill. Small things count when you are getting started on your dream. They can quickly become miracles and victories.

Before Jesus fed the crowd, He asked how much food His disciples could round up. They found a pitifully small amount of fish and bread, but He wasn't concerned with how little they had. He didn't make light of it. He *used* it. Within moments that small lunch fed thousands.

When God commissioned Moses to lead the people of Israel out of Egypt, Moses expressed doubt. "What if they do not believe me or listen to me and say, 'The LORD did not appear to you'?" he asked (Exod. 4:1, NIV). God replied to Moses, "What is that in your hand?" (v. 2, NIV). He was referring to Moses' staff. God called attention to that small, everyday object that Moses may never have considered. From that day on, Moses used that staff to perform many miracles.

There are many other examples throughout the Bible: David had only a few smooth stones and a sling against a giant. Gideon had three hundred men against an army of thousands. But small things led to great victories.

Now the question settles on you: What is in your hand? What can you use to fight the giants that stand in the way of your dream?

1. List the "small things" in your life, including skills, life experiences, connections, or anything else that God might use.

    _____

    _____

    _____

    _____

Prayerfully consider the list, and allow the Holy Spirit to draw your attention to specific things. Ask God if you are overlooking any skill, idea, or something else that would lead toward your dream.

DAY 3

See, I [God] have called by name Bezaleel the son of Uri, the son of Hur, of the tribe of Judah: And I have filled him with the spirit of God, in wisdom, and in understanding, and in knowledge, and in all manner of workmanship, to devise cunning works, to work in gold, and in silver, and in brass, and in cutting of

stones, to set them, and in carving of timber, to work
in all manner of workmanship.

—EXODUS 31:2–5, KJV

Some people think God only cares about skills and gifts like preaching, writing, singing, and other abilities that have an obvious spiritual application. But God calls men and women to all kinds of professions, and every person's work can glorify Him if it is done to the Lord.

In the above passage, God filled men with His spirit and wisdom so they could work with metal and wood. He has also given you wisdom and gifts to excel in a certain way. The Bible says, "So…whatever you do, do it all for the glory of God" (1 Cor. 10:31, NIV).

And whatever you do, whether in word or deed, do it
all in the name of the Lord Jesus, giving thanks to God
the Father through him.

—COLOSSIANS 3:17, NIV

You might be a manicurist, a machine worker, a software programmer, or a travel agent. In each of these jobs, and a thousand other professions, people can work to the glory of God. Your dream does not have to be directly related to ministry. In God's hands, your dream and your skills *are* your ministry.

1. Do you believe your job is your main avenue of ministry? How do you bless others through it?

   _____

   _____

   _____

   _____

Thank God for the skills and wisdom He gave you in your area of gifting, and ask for the wisdom to use them for their highest and best purpose.

DAY 4

> Go, borrow vessels from everywhere, from all your neighbors—empty vessels; do not gather just a few.
>
> —2 KINGS 4:3

One year a flood came and destroyed the church building where my father pastored. When the disaster was over and the waters receded, he decided to move the church to higher ground, so he took me with him to a nearby neighborhood, and we scouted out locations. There was one beautiful lot he wanted to buy, but the church had no money for it, so Dad walked all the way around it and prayed, "God, everywhere my feet walk, I claim this for You." Then he started walking down the block, past the houses near the lot, and as he passed each one he said, "I claim that house, and that house." He got to the end of the block, and there was a warehouse, so he said, "I claim the warehouse while I'm at it." He turned the corner and saw a furniture store and a parking lot behind it, and he claimed them both.

It wasn't long until his church owned every bit of that property, plus the block across the street!

My father planned for greatness. He didn't just kneel on some ugly old piece of property and beg God for it. He expanded his horizon. He prayed with a big vision in his heart.

Right now you are laying the groundwork for the size and scope of your dream. It will probably only grow as big as you plan for it to be. When God is involved, it is your job to gather not "just a few," as Elisha told the widow. Expect and plan for greatness, and God will bless that bigness of vision.

1. What can you do right now to plan big for your dream?

_____

_____

_____

_____

2. Do you sincerely expect God to do great things in your life? If not, why not? What are your excuses?

_____

_____

_____

_____

Pray for great expectations to guide your dreams and plans.

DAY 5

> Without faith it is impossible to please God.
> —HEBREWS 11:6, NIV

I have always followed my dreams even when I didn't have the resources to carry them out. In Davenport, my church would buy buses, and if we ever got into a lean time financially, we didn't back off—we bought more buses!

In Phoenix, we began digging the foundation for a 7,000-seat sanctuary, but workers hit rock and the cost of the dig went from $50,000 to $300,000. We didn't have that kind of money. We didn't have a loan. And yet we were building a $7 million building. What did we do? We kept on digging and building. Today, that "impossible" building has been serving hundreds of thousands of people for more than twenty years.

How do you do great things for God? Through faith. Your dream must never be a slave to your bank account or your understanding of a situation. Your dream should rely on the impossible. It should force you at times to ask, believe, and act beyond what seems logical. It should require faith, which is "the substance of things hoped for, the evidence of things not seen" (Heb. 11:1).

1. What have you done in the past week that required faith?

    _____

    _____

    _____

    _____

2. If Jesus were to assess your faith level, would He say, "O you of little faith" (Matt. 8:26)? Or would He say, "I have not found such great faith, not even in Israel!" (Matt. 8:10). How can you be a person of greater faith?

_____

_____

_____

_____

Consider the time when the father of a sick boy asked Jesus to heal his son. The man told Jesus, "I do believe; help me overcome my unbelief!" (Mark 9:24, NIV). Pray that God would help you to overcome unbelief to be a person of great faith.

DAY 6

> Now that you know these things, you will be blessed if you do them.
>
> —JOHN 13:17, NIV

Promises must be obtained. Faith must be put into action, or it is not faith. But too many dreamers fear the criticism they might receive once they step out. They fear their dreams won't turn out the way they should, and they may look foolish. They want to accomplish great things with no risk involved. And so they don't take action. They hold the dream in their mind and heart, but they never let it grow and expand.

Any person who reaches his or her dream will tell you that it takes plenty of action to get there. In Hebrews 11, we see that the men and women of great faith took action.

- Abel offered a more excellent sacrifice.

- Noah prepared an ark.

- Abraham went out, not knowing where he was going.

- Moses and the Israelites passed through the Red Sea.

- Others subdued kingdoms, worked righteousness, and stopped the mouths of lions.

They were people of action. The Bible warns:

> Do not merely listen to the word, and so deceive yourselves. Do what it says. Anyone who listens to the word but does not do what it says is like a man who looks at his face in a mirror and, after looking at himself, goes away and immediately forgets what he looks like. But the man who looks intently into the perfect law that gives freedom, and continues to do this, not forgetting what he has heard, but doing it—he will be blessed in what he does.
>
> —JAMES 1:22–25, NIV

The point is clear: if you want your dream to be blessed, you must take action. Your dream is no good rattling around inside your head. It must become a tangible reality through the steps you take.

1. How have you taken action to fulfill your dream? List the ways:

    _____

    _____

    _____

    _____

2. What action can you take today?

    _____

    _____

    _____

    _____

Pray that you would be a doer of the Word, not just a hearer.

DAY 7

His divine power has given us everything we need for life and godliness through our knowledge of him who called us by his own glory and goodness.

—2 PETER 1:3, NIV

At times, Christianity can be celebrity-oriented. People say, "If I could get that preacher to pray for me, my needs would be taken care of. If I go to this church conference or that revival meeting, I'll get the answer I need."

People do the same with their dreams: "If I could get that person who has so much money to sign on to my vision, then my dream would be realized."

Such thinking insults God because it ignores the power at work in us. Paul wrote, "I pray that out of his glorious riches he may strengthen you with power through his Spirit in your inner being" (Eph. 3:16, NIV). Paul also wrote:

> To them God has chosen to make known among the Gentiles the glorious riches of this mystery, which is Christ in you, the hope of glory.
>
> —COLOSSIANS 1:27, NIV

These passages point to the power of God at work within us—not outside of us or in someone else's resources. He has given each of us the dignity of having enough power to pursue our own dreams. Not one of us needs to be a beggar. There is power in *you* to fulfill your dreams! Are you using it?

1. Meditate on the above scriptures, reading them in context in your Bible. Do you know the "power through his Spirit in your inner being"? Do you live with "the hope of glory"? How active are these truths in your life? Write your thoughts.

   _____

   _____

   _____

   _____

Pray that "the eyes of your understanding" would be opened and "that you may know what is the hope of His calling, what are the riches of the glory of His inheritance in the saints" (Eph. 1:18).

CHAPTER SEVEN

Dream for a Lifetime

*D*reaming big is exciting and energizing. When you redirect your life so you are going after your dream, your passion gets stirred up, your juices start flowing, and you want to seize every day as if it's the only day that mattered. Your spirit soars, you feel every emotion more deeply, and you realize why you were created by God. Dreaming, and pursuing that dream, is the healthiest, most rewarding thing a person can do.

But in that energy and excitement lurks a danger. A dream can be wrecked by the very passion and energy that fuel it, if the dream is not managed correctly. Dreams are lifelong endeavors. No dream can be achieved in a day or even a year. We must pace ourselves for the long haul, or we run the risk of burning out. Dreams are not a 100-yard dash; they are a long-distance race.

FINISH STRONG

In his book *Finishing Strong: Going the Distance for Your Family*, Steve Farrar recounts the story of three young evangelists who burst onto the American scene in 1945. Their names were Billy Graham, Bron Clifford, and Chuck Templeton. All three were in their mid-twenties, and each rose to quick prominence because of his speaking abilities. Each packed out auditoriums across the country.

One seminary president heard Templeton address an audience of thousands, and he was so impressed that he called him the most talented young preacher in America. Templeton and Graham became close friends and preached together for the Youth for Christ organization. But most people thought Templeton would be the successful one of the two. One magazine featured him in an article and called him "the Babe Ruth of evangelism." The article didn't even mention Graham.

Bron Clifford was tall, dashing, intelligent, and elegant. He was so gifted that he was called the most powerful preacher in the church in centuries. People lined up for hours to hear him. At Baylor University he gave a discourse, and the university president ordered the class bells turned off so that nothing would interfere with Clifford's message. For two and one-half hours the students sat on the edges of their seats, spellbound as he gave a brilliant dissertation. He was so attractive and charming that Hollywood tried to get him to play the lead role in the famous movie *The Robe*.

But a few years later, things had changed for two of these three men. In just five years Chuck Templeton left the ministry, declaring that he no longer believed Jesus Christ was the Son of God. He pursued a career in radio and became a newscaster. The "Babe Ruth" of evangelism gave it up entirely; today, his name resides in the annals of evangelical obscurity. By 1954, Clifford had lost his family, his ministry, and his health because of financial irresponsibility and alcohol abuse. He left his wife and their two Down's syndrome children. At the age of thirty-five, he died in a cheap hotel on the edge of Amarillo, Texas. Some pastors collected enough money to purchase a casket and ship it back east where he was buried in a pauper's cemetery.

Billy Graham, of course, went on to be the best-known, most beloved evangelist of the second half of the twentieth century—a spiritual advisor to seven presidents and one of the most respected men in the world.

Two had sprinted, but one ran the distance race.

Your success in following your dreams won't be judged by how you start but by how you finish.*

The Bible says, "The end of a thing is better than its beginning" (Eccles. 7:8). I learned this as a runner in junior high school. I tried out for the 100-yard dash, but I was not as fast as the rest of the boys. But I had determination, so I began running the mile and winning. Then I ran the 2-mile race. I discovered that if I kept going, I could outlast my opponents, outlast my doubts, and outlast my struggles. All I had to do was set my pace and keep going.

That is a recipe for successful dreaming. Remember the people in high school who seemed so full of promise? The athlete or the gifted speaker, or the one who was voted the most likely to succeed? Where are those people now? Do they have the world by the tail?

---

* Steve Farrar, *Finishing Strong: Going the Distance for Your Family* (Sisters, OR: Multnomah, 1996).

Life is a road that tests your dream. It puts it through hurdles and rocky places. The secret to dreaming for a lifetime is to set a pace and keep it to the very end. What will your dream look like in ten years? Twenty years? Are you ready to go the distance? Are you sprinting or pacing yourself? Is your dream leading you to burnout, or will you finish stronger than you started?

Let me share a few simple strategies to help you finish strong.

Stick to one thing.

I have a friend who runs a business that employs 2,800 people and has a payroll of $1 million a week. He once told me, "Whenever I have invested in a venture outside my own business, I've lost money and failed. I've concluded that when I invest in my own business, it prospers. God gave me this business as the one thing I can do, so I focus on it." This man is one of the most generous men I know, and he has supported ministries in countless ways.

When you scatter your efforts, you scatter your effectiveness, but when you fix your mind on "this one thing," as Paul said in Philippians 3:13, you do service to your dream. Don't get side-tracked by ideas that seem attractive but take you in a different direction. They will dilute your efforts. Stick to the one dream in your heart.

Get a fresh vision of the finish line.

Along the way, keep your vision fresh. It is not enough to have had a vision last week or last year. That vision must be as fresh every day as your morning coffee. It must be renewed, and it will be if you stick to the disciplines we have talked about of praying, praising, Bible reading, communing with the Holy Spirit, and so on. At the time of this writing, I am in my sixties, and I understand that it is just as important, if not more important, for me to have fresh vision now than when I was in my twenties. Every day I lift my eyes above the present situation, and I look at the horizon of my dream. I see the vision and the purpose of all I'm doing in light of God's purposes. The psalmist wrote in Psalm 123:1:

> Unto You I lift up my eyes, O You who dwell in the heavens.

The psalmist also wrote:

> I will lift up my eyes to the mountains.
> —Psalm 121:1, NAS

Take a moment each day to lift your eyes, look at the mountains, get your mind off the small details, and see again the bigger purpose behind your dream.

Don't quit.

Sounds easy, doesn't it? Sometimes it is; sometimes it isn't. The key to not quitting is simply to keep doing what you are doing no matter what life throws at you. You may be in a season of amassing resources, educating yourself, serving someone else's dream, or taking action. Whatever season you are in, do it with all your energy. Don't set the cruise control. Do it purposefully, one step at a time, and don't quit.

In studying the lives of great men in history and in the Bible, I have found there is a particular honor in wanting to quit but not actually quitting. The prophet Jeremiah wanted to quit. He went to the woods, got a little cabin with a fishing hole nearby, and quit the ministry—so to speak. But the Word of God burned in his bones like a fire, and he eventually said, "I cannot constrain myself."

Abraham, the friend of God, the man who walked with God, wanted to quit. He got depressed and left his dream to go to Egypt. But he didn't quit forever, and his dream was fulfilled.

Peter, who walked on water and was the leader of the disciples, wanted to quit. When Jesus was crucified, Peter denied the Lord and even cursed God, and then he ran home to resume his maritime career. But he soon returned to his higher calling.

Thomas, who later died as a martyr, wanted to quit. He would not believe Jesus had risen again.

John the Baptist, whom the Bible calls the greatest man born of a woman, doubted his salvation and wanted to quit.

Noah wanted to quit. Moses wanted to quit. Daniel wanted to quit.

Great preachers like Charles Spurgeon, who built one of the greatest churches of all time, wanted to quit. Martin Luther wanted to quit. Winston Churchill suffered with depression throughout his life and many times wanted to quit. But none of them did.

Every great man I have ever known or read about has considered quitting. That tells us something: wanting to quit is a sign of success. In fact, the more responsibility you have, the more you will want to quit. As a dreamer, you can enjoy the luxury of wanting to quit…but only if you know that you will not quit.

I have wanted to quit all my life. When I ran cross-country as a high school student, the coach ran us up and down hills and valleys, then he would run us up and down the stands, and then we ran wind sprints. I wanted to quit every day, but I never did.

I wanted to quit when I was an evangelist staying in lonely evangelist's quarters all by myself in old creaky churches in West

Texas. There is nothing scarier than an old church in the middle of the night. I wanted to quit and run home, but I never did.

I wanted to quit when I saw my first church, and when people threatened my life because I fought the massage parlors in Davenport. I wanted to quit when newspapers criticized and ridiculed me in Phoenix.

To this day, I want to quit most every Monday morning when the alarm goes off at 5:30 a.m. and I have to get up for prayer. I give myself the luxury of wanting to quit because I know I am not a quitter. David said, "My heart is steadfast" (Ps. 57:7). That is the commitment of a dreamer. We can yearn to quit because we know we never will.

Don't mind the delays.

Many of us think of quitting when our dream is delayed. God often takes us through seasons of hardship on the way to our dream's fulfillment. I don't know of any person who has reached his or her dream without going through very difficult times. Those tough seasons are marked by struggle and stress, tears and sleeplessness. Everything seems to go wrong despite our best efforts. Prayer seems to get us nowhere.

I'm sorry to break it to you, but you cannot pray away God-appointed seasons of struggle. You can claim every promise, quote every scripture, and pray against every obstacle, but if the season is God's idea, it will continue until He stops it. That's because God has a purpose in allowing seasons of fruitlessness. We need those seasons of struggle because they develop our dreams. They destroy pride in our own ability and reinforce our dependency upon God. Many other lessons are learned in those times as well.

Don't be shocked when you find yourself suddenly in a season of struggle. Remember that in the frosty arms of winter, the trees of the forest gain strength. That's when the sap goes deep into the ground and nourishes the roots. When the growing season comes, the tree can handle much more fruit than before.

Springtime always follows winter. Delay is natural. God may work on the dreamer, but He never shelves the dream. The Bible says all who live godly in Christ Jesus will suffer. It says many are the afflictions of the righteous. But Paul calls those very afflictions "light" and "for a moment" (2 Cor. 4:17). Life will always have its broken places, its delays, its struggles, and its conflicts. But when you know you have divine purpose and a divine dream, you can hang on through them all. God doesn't forget who you are. He doesn't forget where you are, or your struggles or specific hardships. Genesis 8:1 says, "But God remembered Noah and all the wild animals and the livestock that were with him in the ark, and he sent a wind over the earth, and the waters receded" (NIV). The Bible says, "For God is not unrighteous to forget your works" (Heb. 6:10, KJV).

God keeps records of every day of your life. He knows your family. He knows your generosity, your work for God, your abilities, and your faith. He knows every hair on your head and every breath you take. More importantly, He knows your dreams, and He knows how best to fulfill them. He will lead you through the right season at the right time. Your job is to keep going forward, even when the dream seems delayed.

GIVE UP SOME DREAMS

That's right. To make it to the end, we must learn which dreams to abandon. If you are like me, when you start dreaming, many different ideas come to mind. One dream spawns another and then another. It's easy to sort some of those dreams out, but others are harder to dismiss. They will seem like long-term dreams, but in the end you will find they detract from your primary dream, and you will have to lay them aside. Dreaming is a lifetime endeavor. Your job is to pay attention to what God is saying to you and give up lesser dreams in favor of greater dreams. For example, I used to lay in bed at night and dream about getting married. I dreamed about having a family, about my children, what I wanted them to be like, what I wanted them to do, how I wanted to love them, and how I wanted them to love me. That dream has happened for me. I am living it right now. It was a dream I saw through to the very end.

But I have abandoned other dreams along the way so I could pursue greater dreams. One of my dreams was to own a house on a golf course with a lake nearby so I could retreat there and watch the ducks fly and fish jump. I intended to retire there. I even bought a piece of property on a golf course in Flagstaff and was ready to build my retirement cottage. But I gave up that dream so I could use my time, energy, and money to build a church in Los Angeles. I sold my beautiful golf course property and got an apartment in downtown Los Angeles. Did I lose one dream? Yes. Did I gain a better one? Absolutely!

Your dreams can and will change as you mature. As you grow closer to God's heart, the things that matter to Him will matter more to you, and that will cause you to see your goals and objectives differently. Your primary destiny and dream will stay the same, but the other goals and ideas you have will come under closer scrutiny as you trim your life down to the one thing you hope to accomplish.

I am convinced that we should never catch up to our dreams. If you accomplish everything you wanted to in life and still have time left over, you need to dream again. Dream bigger and better than before. Never outrun or outlast your dreams.

Let's review what we have learned about reaching our dreams:

- Each person has a dream and a destiny in life. God created you to do something better than anyone else. Not only were you born for a purpose, but also your destiny was all set up before you even knew about it.

- Your dream provides the blueprint for your purpose in life. You can only be truly happy when pursuing your dream.

- Your dream will only make sense when you have given your life to Jesus Christ.

- God wants your dreams and desires to be fulfilled.

- Dreaming takes courage to break free of past failures, satisfaction, and fears.

- Dreams must be cultivated with prayer, perfected praise, Bible study, and fellowship.

- Dreams must be multiplied by generosity, service, love, and readiness to share Jesus with other people.

- The Holy Spirit is your dream partner. A daily relationship with Him will revolutionize your life and propel you toward your dream.

- There is a miracle in your house to make your dream possible. You have everything you need to start achieving your dream.

- Dreams are lifelong endeavors. You must set your pace and never quit.

Now it's your turn—it's time to go for those dreams! It's time to take action, set your pace, step onto the playing field, and let people know that from now on, you are pursuing the dream God has planted in your heart. This is your day, and if you follow it through to the end, the Bible says you will experience the greatest moment imaginable when you step into heaven and into the arms of Jesus Himself, who will tell you:

> Well done, good and faithful servant; you were faithful over a few things, I will make you ruler over many things.
>
> —MATTHEW 25:21

So let it be for each one of us. Dreamers, let's go for it!

Study Guide Questions

1. Discuss a time when you experienced burnout on the path to your dream. How did you get back on track?

   _____

   _____

   _____

   _____

2. How do you pace yourself in life?

   _____

   _____

   _____

   _____

3. In what areas of your life are you concentrating your efforts? Out of those areas, what one area do you perform your best and should concentrate on the most? Explain.

   _____

   _____

   _____

   _____

4. How do you refresh your vision? What habits do you have for getting the big picture?

    _____

    _____

    _____

    _____

5. How often do you feel like quitting? Have you ever quit, thinking it was for good?

    _____

    _____

    _____

    _____

6. Talk about a season of delay you have been through. What were the results of that season?

    _____

    _____

    _____

    _____

7. What dreams have you given up for the sake of better ones? How has your dream been refined, even in the past few weeks? Has God changed your dream?

_____

_____

_____

_____

8. What do you need to do to finish strong?

_____

_____

_____

_____

Reflections

DAY 1

Read and review the chapter material.

DAY 2

> You were running a good race. Who cut in on you and
> kept you from obeying the truth?
>
> —GALATIONS 5:7, NIV

A woman told me years ago, "I don't want to get close to God. I just want to get close enough to get to heaven. When I went to high school, I wanted to make straight Cs, because if I made straight Fs I would fail, but if I made straight As, people would expect more of me. That's the way I am with God. If I fail Him, I'll make straight Fs and go to hell. But if I do too much for Him, He might expect more of me and ask me to do things I don't want to."

Each of us has to set a pace as we progress toward our dreams. That pace should not be so fast that we quickly run out of energy, and it should not be so slow that we waste our potential. It should be sustainable and require as much as we can give over the long term.

The woman I quoted set her pace well below her abilities because she was selfish, lazy, and fearful. She did the opposite of what Paul instructed when he said:

> Do you not know that in a race all the runners run,
> but only one gets the prize? Run in such a way as to

get the prize. Everyone who competes in the games goes into strict training. They do it to get a crown that will not last; but we do it to get a crown that will last forever.

—1 CORINTHIANS 9:24–25, NIV

I would rather discover that I am running too fast than too slow. I want my pace to be at the top of my abilities. I want to give every bit of my energy in service to God.

1. What is your current pace in pursuing your dream? How does it need to change, if at all?

_____

_____

_____

_____

2. Have you ever tired out from going at too fast of a pace? When? Have you ever been bored because your pace was too slow? Consider these experiences and write your thoughts.

_____

_____

_____

_____

Pray that you would run "to get the prize"—a crown that will last forever.

DAY 3

Brothers, I do not consider myself yet to have taken hold of it. But one thing I do: Forgetting what is behind and straining toward what is ahead, I press on toward the goal to win the prize for which God has called me heavenward in Christ Jesus.

—PHILIPPIANS 3:13–14, NIV

When I turned fifty, I began to consider my future. My father had died at age sixty-seven. I began to wonder how many years were left for me. God answered that question with a question to me.

He spoke to my heart one day, "Are you going to look back some day and say, 'What if?' 'What if I had given my money, time, and energy to God?' Are you going to have regrets?"

I got on my knees and prayed, "God, I may not have the potential other men have, but when I die, I would like people to say that I came the closest to reaching my potential of any man who ever lived."

Almost twenty years later, I sometimes wonder if I should have prayed that prayer! It has taken my life, my energy, my time—every ounce and more of what I have. But I know that in this life and the next I will never regret devoting my life to this one thing.

1. In your own words, describe the one thing for which you are living.

   _____

   _____

   _____

   _____

2. At the end of your life, what would you regret most? How can you avoid having any regrets?

   _____

   _____

   _____

   _____

Pray that you would understand how to live so that you have no regrets.

DAY 4

> But those who wait on the LORD shall renew their strength; they shall mount up with wings like eagles.
>
> —ISAIAH 40:31

One day I was speaking to an Australian minister friend, telling him what a great country he came from and how much I enjoyed the sights, sounds, and people there. He listened for a moment and then said, "Australia is a wonderful country. I was born there, and I have lived there most of my life, but America is a magnificent country. What sets it apart from any other place in the world is that America has a vision. America has a dream. Americans are the most positive dreamers in the world."

I love living in a country with that kind of reputation! But I believe his assessment should be true of Christians, too. We should have a knack for always seeing fresh opportunities, new vistas, and unexplored possibilities. We should be the pioneers, inventors, and creative forces in our industries.

To stay ahead of the game, you must have fresh vision along the way. If you keep your eyes on the process, you will get discouraged. But if you refresh your vision every day, it will sustain you. Getting fresh vision may be a matter of reading or researching in the area of your dream. It may mean taking a break to go to the mountains, the lake, or the ocean to get your mind on the big picture again.

Do what you need to do to recapture the original vision.

1. How do you keep your vision fresh? What works for you? List some ideas.

    _____

    _____

    _____

    _____

2.   If you have lost your vision of the big picture—of the horizon—what can you do today to bring it back?

_____

_____

_____

_____

Pray that God would remind you to lift your eyes to the One who is enthroned in the heavens so that your vision stays fresh.

DAY 5

> Count it all joy when you fall into various trials, knowing that the testing of your faith produces patience. But let patience have its perfect work, that you may be perfect and complete, lacking nothing.
>
> —JAMES 1:2–4

As a young pastor, I went through a phase where I wanted to quit every time the going got rough. I would dwell on the reasons for my discouragement and tell my wife, "I don't have to be a pastor my whole life. I don't have to stay a slave to other people's opinions and criticisms. I could get out of the ministry and do something completely different." I am sure you know what I am talking about.

I went through that cycle over and over again, visualizing myself in other professions. But after a while I realized it was just a fantasy. I wouldn't quit. I wasn't a quitter, and God didn't want me to quit. If I stopped preaching or pastoring just because I felt like it, I wouldn't be consistent in anything I did. I would zigzag between professions, and my life would come to nothing.

Today, I allow myself the luxury of wanting to quit because I know I never will! I get strange comfort from knowing that I could quit, if I choose to, but that I won't because I'm not a quitter.

Your dream will lead you into places and times of life when you want nothing more than to quit and get out of the dream business altogether. You will daydream about taking up another trade. You will imagine the peace and harmony of soul you would feel having escaped the demands of your dream. King David was stuck in a tough situation, and he said, "Oh that I had wings like a dove! for then would I fly away, and be at rest" (Ps. 55:6, KJV).

But deep down you will know that the purpose of trials is to produce patience and perfection, as the apostle James wrote in today's scripture.

You can think about quitting—but don't quit!

1. When was the last time you thought about quitting your dream? Why?

   _____

   _____

   _____

   _____

2.   Have you actually quit your dream before? What was the result? How did you get back on track?

_____

_____

_____

_____

Ask God for grace to keep going, even when quitting seems to be the easy way out.

DAY 6

> For the vision is yet for an appointed time;
> But at the end it will speak, and it will not lie.
> Though it tarries, wait for it;
> Because it will surely come,
> It will not tarry.
>
> —HABAKKUK 2:3

When I first entered the ministry at age sixteen, teenage evangelists were all the rage. Some were filling auditoriums and preaching to thousands. They had great campaigns that touched cities and brought them national recognition.

I was a teenage evangelist during that time, but I wasn't in the big cities preaching to thousands. I was in the deserts of west Texas preaching to fifty or one hundred. God gave me some "success," but nothing like what others were experiencing. My dream of shaking the world for God was delayed, no matter how hard I tried to make it happen.

Delay is a natural, if unpleasant, part of reaching your dream. It feels as if God is saying, "No. No. No." You may not understand why; it may seem as if He is toying with you, but in God's eyes the "delay" is a time of preparation. If you do not grow through it, you cannot reach your dream.

Every hero in the Bible went through lengthy times of delay. Paul was out of the spotlight for a decade or more before he began preaching and writing letters to brand-new churches throughout Asia Minor.

Moses tended sheep in the desert for forty years before God tapped him to lead Israel out of Egypt.

Abraham had to wait twenty-five years for the child of promise to be born.

Sadly, many if not most of the teenage evangelists of my youth are no longer in ministry, and some are not even walking with God. Perhaps they never had their "delay" time of learning lessons to sustain them. I am thankful now that God stuck me in the desert and shielded me from early "success."

If you find yourself in a time of delay, rejoice, work hard, and draw close to God. Soon enough the delay will end, and all the lessons you learned will be put into practice.

1. When was your most recent period of delay? Are you in one now? How do you know it's a God-ordained time of preparation?

   _____

   _____

   _____

   _____

Pray that God's purpose in the times of delay would be fully accomplished in you.

DAY 7

> Again, the kingdom of heaven is like a merchant looking for fine pearls. When he found one of great value, he went away and sold everything he had and bought it.
>
> —MATTHEW 13:45–46, NIV

I had a decision to make.

For nearly a decade, I had pastored a fast-growing church in Davenport, Iowa. Four thousand people attended each week, and we were one of the most watched churches in America. I thought I had reached my dream.

But then God interrupted that success and made it clear I was to go to Phoenix and consider becoming the pastor of a church of only two hundred people. The church had been through ten years of trouble and instability. The last thing I wanted was to give up what I had worked for in Davenport to go to a small church halfway across the country!

But that's exactly what I did, because God made it clear my dream had been fulfilled in Davenport and a new one was being born in Phoenix.

Sometimes following our dreams means giving up things that we count precious. God may give you success in one area and then move you into another, giving you a new dream to pursue. As His servants, we must obey. After all, our dreams are not about self-gratification but about doing what God wants us to do. He is our dream-giver and dream-guider.

My new dream in Phoenix went way beyond what I had accomplished in Davenport. God brought opportunities into my life that I hadn't even anticipated. I am so glad I gave up one dream to follow another!

1. Has God ever asked you to stop pursuing one dream in order to pursue another? Explain.

———————————————————————

———————————————————————

———————————————————————

———————————————————————

2. What are you willing to give up so you can reach your dream?

_____

_____

_____

_____

Ask God if you are pursuing "outdated" or lesser dreams. Ask for wisdom in seeing which dream you should be pursuing at this time.

DAY 50

The last forty-nine days have been a time of dreaming and discovery, a time of evaluating your life and reason for living, and a time for planning your future based on the dreams God has placed in your heart. You have learned about cultivating your dream; how to know which dreams are of God; how to discover a miracle in your house; how to dream with the Holy Spirit; how to dream for a lifetime, and much more.

I hope that you have faithfully attended—and participated in—your study groups. I hope you have taken full advantage of the devotional portion of this book and have reflected on your life, your dreams, and what God wants you to do from this day forward. Today is your own personal Day of Pentecost—Day 50—on that journey to fulfilling your dream. It is a day of changing direction, if needed. I encourage you to set this day apart, taking time to fast, pray, and meditate upon what you learned over the last forty-nine days. In the course of the day, set you heart toward the new course you will take toward your dreams.

1. In the space provided, describe what the Holy Spirit revealed to you today about fulfilling the dream.

    _____

    _____

    _____

    _____

2. Think about the areas that you committed to work on and change in your life. In a few brief points, write down and reaffirm your plan to work toward that goal.

    _____

    _____

    _____

    _____

REACHING YOUR DREAMS

For small groups, church outreaches, and personal study

This inspiring journey to spiritual discovery has been designed to be used also as an outreach tool for churches and small groups.

In addition to this book, an entire church outreach program is available; it includes video teaching segments by Pastor Tommy Barnett on DVD to be used in weekly home groups; sermon outlines and transcripts; and video and drama segments to complement services during the seven weeks of outreach.

Additional helps include neighborhood door hangers, invitation cards, campaign resources, training, and much more.

For more information on using this book as a small group study or churchwide outreach, visit www.toreachyourdreams.com or call 602-867-7117 and ask for "Reaching Your Dreams."

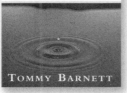

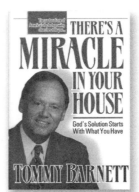

Strang Communications, the publisher of both Charisma House and *Charisma* magazine, wants to give you 3 FREE ISSUES of our award-winning magazine.

Since its inception in 1975, *Charisma* magazine has helped thousands of Christians stay connected with what God is doing worldwide.

Within its pages you will discover in-depth reports and the latest news from a Christian perspective, biblical health tips, global events in the body of Christ, personality profiles, and so much more. Join the family of *Charisma* readers who enjoy feeding their spirit each month with miracle-filled testimonies and inspiring articles that bring clarity, provoke prayer, and demand answers.

To claim your **3 free issues** of *Charisma,* send your name and address to: Charisma 3 Free Issue Offer, 600 Rinehart Road, Lake Mary, FL 32746. Or you may call 1-800-829-3346 and ask for Offer # 93FREE. This offer is only valid in the USA.

---

www.charismamag.com